Rarely, and with such rawness, do we get to see inside the mind and heart of a precious soul fighting for a life once lived. With courage and grace Colleen shares her pilgrimage as she breathes, first tentatively then tenaciously, new dreams into a broken life. Riveting and reflective reading awaits...

I have known Colleen my entire life. We could have never guessed that as small children with only four years separating us, and family ties binding us, that we were destined to be part of each other's falling and flourishing odysseys.

She is rebellious and relentless in the most beautiful of ways; attributes many women in out lineage share with fierce gratitude. So it is no surprise that in the harrowing halls of UCLA Medical Center she fought, or in the suffocating pain she persevered, or amidst hopeless odds she created a new life. What is surprising is that she can tell her story. More than a story she has shown us what it takes, thoughts and tools, to reclaim and refresh her own life, and then breathe that new life into her family. She has been renewed by her grit, her faith, her family and friends and the simplicity of profound grace. Walk with her through a fractured life into one flourishing with possibility and you will see the same is possible for you.

Dr. Brenda Wilkins
Senior Faculty, Center for Creative Leadership

Colleen is living her legacy on her terms and creating massive change. Colleen is one of the most inspiring people I know; she is exactly what brave looks like. She is a no excuse and roll up your sleeve woman whose drive and compassion is clear every step of the way.

Jo Dibblee, author of "Frock Off—Living Undisguised"
Readers' Favorite Bronze Medalist 2014

I carry your book with me in my purse as a symbol of your talk you gave that filled my heart and inspired me that if the strength of the human spirit could choose to heal, I too could create miracles.

Roni-lil Shapka, Vector Marketing

Colleen's story is amazing! I was absolutely stuck to the edge of my seat at her presentation in. To me she is the definition of determination and a true testament of the power of ones will power!

Brenda Davidson, Past President of Executive Women's International, Calgary, Alberta

I read your book Colleen...it truly is an inspirational story... would love to hear you present it! What were you saying about stories in LA always being made into movies?? Why not?!

Dina Michetti-Ehnes

HOW I TRAINED MYSELF BACK TO LIFE

BREATHE

A MEMOIR OF LIFE AFTER BRAIN TRAUMA

COLLEEN HIERATH

COLLEEN HIERATH
CONSULTING

Cover design, interior book design,
and eBook design
by Blue Harvest Creative
www.blueharvestcreative.com

Editing by BHC Staff Editor Bailey Karfelt

Please note: This book was edited to the author's requirements. Due to the nature of the subject, text is written as requested and may contain certain grammatical errors. These errors are intentional.

BREATHE

Published by
Colleen Hierath Consulting

ISBN-13: 978-1511778626
ISBN-10: 1511778628

Visit the author at:

Website: *www.colleenhierath.com*
Facebook: *colleen.hierath*
Twitter: *www.twitter.com/ColleenHierath*
YouTube: *www.youtube.com/channel/UCIPN7b6F4bNu4ZbN3YyONgg*

Visit the author's website
by scanning the QR code.

DISCLAIMER

The author designed the information to represent her opinions about the subjects disclosed. The reader must weigh carefully all aspects of any business decision before making any changes in their business or life. The author obtained the information contained through personal experience and the experiences of her career.

The author speaks from her perspective and experience. The author disclaims any liability, loss or risk incurred by individuals who act on the information contained herein. The author believes the device presented here is sound, but readers cannot hold Colleen Hierath or Colleen Hierath Consulting responsible for either the actions they take or the result of those actions.

TABLE OF CONTENTS

BREATHE

...FOREWORD

When Colleen asked me to write the forward for her book, I hesitated. Not because I was not honored, but because I truly wondered how I could capture the essence of BREATHE in a few short paragraphs.

After having the privilege to read her manuscript, and to get to know Colleen personally, I was desperate to make a change in the way I was currently thinking. I thought I was doing ok, but I could clearly see where I was being held back in the battlefield of my mind.

Here is a woman who had earned the right to belong to the "victim club of life," but chose to rise above it. NOTHING I have gone through in my life even begins to touch the smallest part of her story. It sounds cliché, but the truth is—if she can go from being broken and broken down (literally and figuratively) and rise to this fully functioning, effervescent, dynamic, passionate, purpose-filled woman—then I have nothing to stop me from being the best I can be! Am I right?

It is a story clearly marked by the scripture, "I can do all things through Christ who strengthens me."

The steps she took are duplicable, meaning you can find victory in your life too. Her steps are transferable. You can use these same steps to conquer any trouble, financial, relationship, spiritual and in health. It covers every perceivable tragedy out there. Her steps are teachable, meaning you will have new tools that you can share with others as you heal and grow; as you change from victim to victory.

My new question in life when I come against seemingly insurmountable odds is "Kathleen, what is the alternative? What if I don't make the effort today? What if I don't do the first step first?"

I think that if you could see what it looks like to give up, hide, or run—it will haunt you for the rest of your life. Do what Ms. Hierath did and use this tool to "keep on, keepin' on."

When the alternative screams out "my life will be over!—I am living in Hell!"—scream louder—"I WILL OVERCOME!"

Kathleen D. Mailer, Founder, Editor-In-Chief of "Today's Businesswoman Magazine," Author and Professional Speaker

DEDICATION

I dedicate my book to God. Thanks for a second life.
I also dedicate this book to my children Haley, Shea and Quinn.

BREATHE

...MY STORY, PART I

HOW MY STORY BEGAN

AUGUST 1, 1988

Great Day, only two pukes! I had to wear the red dress again, I'm down to two dresses that I can fit into. There isn't anyone in the entire company that is pregnant, feel totally out of sync. Everyone is wondering if I am going to abandon them, so I never talk about it. Frankly I am not sure about my plans. I have not made any commitments. I hope my work will allow me the freedom to work part time from home.

I don't think I can have it all.

But I have invested a lot into my career.

But I really am committed to raising this baby. My Haley.

Who knows?

AFTERNOON

Love work, phones ringing, deals closing. I am at my best on speed dial. Wow, look how my feet have swollen, my hands too. My ring finger is turning purple. I need to go to a jeweler and get those rings off my finger or I will lose it.

3 PM

"I don't care about the pain, just cut these off."
With twisted rings in hand I head to the mall to buy some shoes that will fit. Wow, size nine! What happened to my size seven feet? This is a bad day.

AUGUST 5

Dreaming about not eating and puking. Had to pull over on the way home from work and get chicken from El Pollo Loco. Ate the chicken in the car, almost ate the box.

EXERCISE

Total Surrender, walked two miles. I never walk, but I was running so slow that I could walk faster. It feels like defeat. My doctor is a runner and has been supportive. Running has made me tough. I admire tough. Love to run the Santa Monica Mountains and Griffith Park. I have run my whole life. Running is like flying, soaring. I don't stress because I run. Running fuels my flame. I run to the beat of a different drum, a strong beat. I love to run The Strand at Manhattan Beach. I can't wait to get back at it.

I was thinking about motivation today. You are either motivated or not. No one else can motivate you. I like to set goals and achieve them. I like to do my best. I never quit. I am grateful my parents instilled this in me.

AUGUST 6

Totally freaked out some construction workers when I opened up the car door and hurled my guts out. They kept yelling at me, asking if they could help. Rather embarrassing. I had to make a fast getaway. I had better carry a bag on my lap now for these emergencies.

Knees are killing me; I was puffing last night while putting the clothes away. Somehow I have gained fifty pounds, even though I puke all the time, still exercise and can only eat five kinds of food. My due date is August 22 so it won't be long before my body will be back to normal. My clothes look so dorky.

AUGUST 19

It's my thirtieth birthday. I have been looking forward to thirty my whole life. We are going for a drive on Sunday to look at some property to build a weekend home. Can't wait. I just know the best years are coming. Loving Life. I remember thinking about thirty when I was younger. I knew I would be doing something interesting and living somewhere interesting, and I am. Just getting by or just showing up in life was never attractive to me. I think at thirty I am going to discover something exciting to do next. May Day, May Day, My Ship is Going Down.

AUGUST 21, SUNDAY

Angels, I see angels…. I am going to die.
OH HOLY NO!
My guardian angel! Oh God, help me. I am not prepared to die. Prayers are leaping from my silent mouth.

I have known since I was five years old that I was going to die in a car accident. I have had dreams about it my whole life that I tucked away and never contemplated. But the sound of bending metal and screeching tires brings it all back to me. I am in the fight for my life. All in one second, the moment of truth is here. Destiny is crashing into me.

Angels are standing guard over me and Haley. I see their images. They have rushed to my side in such speed that they are a blur. Two white streaks of hope. I feel their hope and comfort, but I am afraid.

Boom. I snap to attention. I must stay conscious or we are going to die. More prayers are escaping my lips. I am bleeding vaginally, I am on the floor, and my arm is broken. It hurts. *PAIN.* I need Haley out of me *now!*

The time is now. *Pain. Fierce. Unbelievable.*

Trying to stay conscious as the firemen are cutting the door off so they can get me out. If I go into shock I will die. My husband, Wes, is alive and in shock. My life is spinning of control. I am totally, uncomfortably aware of everything that is happening around me. People are getting out of their cars to help. People are coming out of their homes. Strangers are by my side. Angels are by my side. I am going to die on Sunset Boulevard today.

They are strapping me onto some nasty hard board and putting me in the ambulance. Please take me to Santa Monica Hospital. That is where I planned to give birth. But they keep saying UCLA Medical Center. Please, please not there, it can't be that serious.

I can hear the police escort. Of course we need one; I know how chaotic beach traffic is on a Sunday afternoon. This is freaking me out, because I know that we have to be driving down the median in order to get through the bumper to bumper traffic on the PCH. I can feel the ambulance swerve to the left and I know we are on the wrong side of the road. This is too stressful for me.

I can't take the pain that has taken my voice away. Praying. I hear them all talking over the radio; the paramedics are reporting my condition to UCLA. They are saying the mother has no vitals and they will try to save the baby. Hello! My eyes are open. We just drove past Santa Monica Hospital, past my dreams, headed to the 405. Please not UCLA.

I am alive. Can't anyone hear or see me?

OK, this has got to be a bad dream. There are at least fifty people gowned in this operating room. Now I am scared. Doctors everywhere. This can't be happening. No one is talking to me. *Oh!* They are cutting off my clothes in front of everyone! They are slicing open my stomach. You have got to be kidding me. This cannot be real. I'm alive down here. Where are the drugs? I am not dead. What is going on here?

PAIN. Unbearable pain. It feels like a cold cement coffin is crushing me and I am going to die from the pressure. The pressure is the pain. I am trying to hold the coffin up so that I am not crushed. I can't even scream, because the pain has taken my voice away.

Trying to remove myself from the pain, going to a meadow filled with wild flowers. Trying to escape. Got to stay coherent and present; must participate, must stay in the game. This is the Super Bowl of my life. Release the pain and go to courage. Live or die.

I am not closing my eyes.

I will die.

Courage, help me.

I am so cold. I feel death. One blink away. One breath away. Defeat is not acceptable.

May Day, May Day.

I can't die. I am not ready. Help me please! I feel sickened. I am praying. More, there was more. Holding on to my soul. I am not ready, I need more time. Struggling…don't take me, no not yet.

SCREAMING NO!!!!!!

Revelation.

Hello God, it's me, Colleen.

In my heart, my mind, my soul, my body. "The choice is yours, if you choose to live, you will have to fight for everything you get or you can close your eyes and it will all be over."

"I choose to fight."

Breathe.

And God saved my life.

"Mrs. Hierath, it's a girl."

I exhale and close my eyes.

My life is in God's hands. But I must participate. No other chances. I feel peace at this moment, split seconds after agonizing, truthful death. What a terrifying experience. God called me on the truth of his creation of me. There was more for me to do. Why didn't I know? And now I am going to have to fight for everything I get.

SAME DAY—LONG DAY

OK, now I am pissed. Don't come at me with those electric paddles. I am alive. Look at me, my eyes are open. Can't you tell my soul has not left my body? No way am I going now. Death, get away from me. God wants me to live. You can't have me.

Fine then, watch this! I push the doctor off my chest, and nobody is zapping me. I will make it through this, too. I don't want those vibrations. Hitting the wall. Body don't fail me now.... Breathe.

What do I do next? Keep eyes open, breathe, think, focus, and remove the pain. REMOVE THE PAIN. I feel like I am in a boxing match with death. Why are the doctors not seeing me? Can't someone see that I am alive?

HEMORRHAGING—DYING

Why are you tying my arm down? I'm trying to let you know I am alive. I am in the game. I am not on the sidelines here. I'm on the court.

Great, now they have tied down my good arm and the other one is broken and in some space age contraption. The nerve of them. I want to kick, fight, pinch, bite, scream, anything I can consider, to keep those paddles away from me.

This day just keeps getting worse. Now the priest is administering the last sacraments to me. I must be in real deep ****. But I feel great peace that he is here, at the window of my death and life. Someone else is praying for me.

DÉJÀ VU

Why are these people doing more surgery? How much worse can this day get? Where are the drugs, why can't they knock me out? This is not the way it is supposed to go. Everyone is at a masquerade ball in gowns and green masks.

What time is it?

LATER

Again, oh no, not again.

You have got to be kidding me, surgery again. I am in a war zone fighting for my life and future. Can I survive? I am dodging bullets everywhere. What condition is my condition in? What day is this? What month is this? Where am I exactly?

Are Haley and Wes alive or dead?

MAYBE AUGUST 22

Does anyone know what time it is?

This is what zero feels like. This has been a hard day and night. I am alive, right? I am so tired. I am alive, after being resuscitated three times, and I have twenty-two IVs coming out of my body. Or is that going into my body? I am on some life support breathing thing and dialysis for my kidneys, and I think I am in a coma.

Nobody is talking to me. I hear fear and worry in everyone's voices. It's dark in here. It's like being at the end of a long dark tunnel and I can barely hear the people at the other end. I feel like staying here because I am so tired. I can't muster the energy to respond. I need rest. I need peace.

I am in a big mess and I have got to do something about this.

I am so afraid to breathe on my own. I can hear the machines beeping and pumping. I panic and then they panic when it beeps. Fix it please, quick. What if I can't live without these machines?

I feel prayers, I can tell that people know about me. I can feel their prayers. I can close my eyes now.

I feel HOPE nearby.

SOME DAY LATER

I can picture her face, her long black hair. I see her bouncing up to me with her hair flying. She is four. She is smiling. She is my Haley.

ANOTHER DAY

I can hear Wes begging to let him know that I hear him. I wiggle a thumb. He knows.

Where do I start? What do I have going for me?

I have HOPE. But I am in a fog. I have used all my muster up.

SOME DAYS LATER

I think I am out of the coma, but it doesn't feel very different. I never slept in the coma, and I am so tired. I can see now. Wes is battered, panicked and exhausted.

I have no expectations. Maybe I will be bedridden for the rest of my life, but at least I am alive.

How many days have I been lying here? I see my parents for the first time. They are sad and worried. I need them to take over for me. I am empty because there is no power left in the source. From where does the grace to live come from?

HOPE, are you still there?

AUGUST...MAYBE SEPTEMBER

I am so thirsty. I need a bath. I am covered in blood, and my hair is gross. ICU is like a war zone. MedStar keeps bringing in patients who are on the edge of death. Not a great peer group. It's like a war zone in here. I can't rest because there are so many people and doctors coming and going.

I can't see my body. I don't know what is happening with it. I am in unbelievable pain. I can't move any body part. I have one pillowcase draped over my abdomen and one across my breasts. That's it. What I can see of my arms is that they are mostly black and a bit purple. I am burning up. Heat is radiating off me. My left breast is three times bigger than my right with ice packs on it. I have drains on my abdomen and breasts, pouring the bruised, bad blood out of me. I am drenched in blood. I must be bleeding to death. Why can't they help me?

I hear the medical students talk about the buttons sewn on both sides of my abdomen to help stabilize it. I hear them talk about staples, the central lines on my wrists, neck, groin and ankle, each with tubes coming out. I feel like Frankenstein.

ANOTHER DAY

I can see my knees today. They look like a wise guy took a bat them. Dialysis is exhausting. I think they gave me morphine before it. It is sucking me dry. Please kidneys, I need you.

I am hallucinating. I am watching my fingernails grow. Every dream is about an earthquake, wind storm, or some scheme I have to get myself out of this hospital. I can't stop the hallucinations. They are frightening and real. I am paranoid. I think they are not paying attention to me.

Wes stuck a picture of Haley on the Kleenex box. I don't think they know about my vision. They don't know I am seeing double and triple everything.

At least I know she is alive. I have to leave her in the thoughts and prayers of others until I commit to living or dying. I am still in Death Valley. Somebody take over for me. I am so worried, I have so much anxiety.

Please don't let the sun go down on me.

MAYBE SEPTEMBER

I hope life begins at forty. Thirty sucks. Still haven't slept. I figure if I am awake, I am alive. Sister morphine, please turn this into a dream.

Still can't talk. Can't move any body parts. Why? I don't think I am paralyzed; I feel pain everywhere. I am stressed, I need a run. Somebody get me my running shoes! I want out of this joint.

DAY AFTER DAY

No sleep. A nurse gave me a writing pad. I can't remember how to spell.

The doctors arrive in teams: Ortho, OB, Haematology, Trauma, GYN, Renal, Respiratory, etc., on to infinity. I am outnumbered. I am the only one on my team. I need to score some points for my side.

I know the grave position I am still in. Hemo doctor is here constantly. Apparently I lost thirteen units of blood and all of my body fluids and Haley's fluids got into my system. That accounts for all those bags hanging above my head. Makes sense now.

Thank goodness the head of the UCLA trauma unit was in the hospital on a hot August Sunday afternoon. What are the odds of that? My destiny and his met on that day. I think he probably got an A+ in medical school. He has saved my life over and over again. Eternally grateful to that doctor, and all of the others. Thank goodness the ambulance took me to UCLA.

POSSIBLY SEPTEMBER

What a production, it's like a Fellini movie! The logistics are overwhelming. It takes eight people to lift me into the cardiac chair; something about the dead weight concept. Could also be that with all the fluids being pumped into me, the pregnancy weight, and the fact that my kidneys are not working, I am bloated beyond recognition and weigh a ton.

Everyone is coming out into the hall to see the "dead woman walking." Very unsettling. Way too public for me. I am in trauma and want to be alone. I am wheeled into a room to see Haley for the first time. Someone puts my hand on Haley and her heartbeat slows down. She calms.

Haley, I am here. I am so sorry.

She is hooked up to too many machines and half her head is shaved, with wires coming out of it. I know she is in jeopardy. This is all I can take.

Losing another piece of my broken heart.

MUST BE SEPTEMBER

Got moved out of the ICU MASH unit today. I saw myself in the mirror. It's bad, really bad. My face is not bruised but it is so white, a whiter shade of pale. My eyes are puffy with dark circles and my hair is sticking out everywhere. I can see the arm contraption that is keeping my arm up above my body to keep the swelling down. It's not working. My hand is purple and very swollen, and they keep cutting open the cast to expand it.

One of my OB/GYN doctors from Santa Monica came by. She held my hand and cried. I need to heal. I have to get a grip on this situation. I am going to decide how this story ends. I will beat the odds.

ANOTHER DAY

Another trip to NICU to see Haley. It takes all day to get me ready to go down to see Haley. The nurse is down there in my place. She is trying to put Haley on a pillow on my lap so as not to hurt my wounds. I really can't do this. I am just too weak. This is so sad. She can't suck from a bottle. I am not happy.

Parents left today. I wonder if I will ever see them again. Feeling alone, not sleeping yet, barely communicating, just scribbling some kind of words on the whiteboard they gave me to write on since I can't talk.

DEFINITELY SEPTEMBER

When did I forget how to walk? This must be a bad dream.

Some crazed Physio came in today and said it was time to *walk*. I haven't even lifted a leg or rolled over. I don't think anyone realizes I don't remember how to move. I am too weak to talk, but maybe I can run over her foot with my walker! That will stop all this craziness.

Trying to send signals from my brain to my legs is hurting. I have to think and think and think some more. Where in my brain, body and soul is the knowledge about moving my legs and walking?

With great exhausting effort and grace, I moved.

SOME DAY

My day was so busy. Now that I am eating, nothing is getting between me and my food.

There I am, lying on the bed pan, hooked up to dialysis with the nurse sitting beside me, a janitor mopping the floor and the second tier med students checking out my wounds while I eat. In walks the head of the Trauma Team. He sees what is going on and takes them all out into the hall and scolds them for being so insensitive. I think someone got a B minus today.

Actually all of them are terrific. I thank them for their efforts in saving my life.

Let's focus on getting my kidneys to work. One thing at a time. Focus.

My head is getting clearer. I am realizing that my life will never be the same and that I am clearly not the same person. Enlightenment, please find me.

SOME OTHER DAY

Shoot, they left me in the basement waiting for a transport porter to take me back to my room. I was just here for some x-rays. I don't have any water and I am burning up. I still can't talk and yell at anyone. I am afraid I have been misplaced. *Help!*

Nurses are too busy to give me a bath today. My family looks after my bath for me and helps me to eat. Today I get a new airbag bed so that I don't get bed sores.

Hand is so purple. They keep cutting open the cast. Pain is constant, everywhere. I feel like I am going to be crushed by concrete. It is so heavy I can hardly breathe.

SEPTEMBER SOMETIME

The doctor with the paddles who I pushed off my chest came in today to tell me how I had scared him when I did that. What about me? I was scared. He tells me I can order off the menu reserved for the seventh floor celebrities. Apparently my dying and dying and dying has given me enough status to order lobster in the hospital. The coach of the UCLA Bruins Football Team has dedicated a game to me. I guess we have the same Orthopedic. It helps that Wes works at UCLA and knows the Chancellor.

ANOTHER DAY IN PARADISE

The constant pain I am is starting to break me down. Surviving the C-section without drugs used up all my bravery and pain tolerance. It doesn't matter how many drugs they give me now, the pain doesn't leave me.

MORNING

Asked my first visitor to come and see me. Ev suffered her own tragedy by losing her son in a random shooting a year ago. I need her strength. I don't think I talked. I just felt her strength and compassion. I knew that she knew I was beginning a new chapter in life too. We will embark down this road together.

PM

Reset my arm. Sickening pain. Pain threshold is gone. Dreaming of Jimmy Buffet's Margarita-ville. I just want a beach, sunshine, solitude, peace and safety to watch the tide roll in. Dreaming about going home. It's OK if I never walk again. I'll just be happy to get home. I'll put my mind elsewhere.

SEPTEMBER, DAY 19

Made it home.

Wes on crutches, me in a wheelchair and Haley drugged, bruised but cute as could be. It took the planning of a Swiss watchmaker. The ride on the 405 freeway was difficult. I held a pillow to my abdomen so it would not jiggle or jar. My sister Margie was in charge of knowing how many steps in the trip, when to rest and transporting me up a flight of stairs to our condo.

My home is chaos; family members have been in and out. Every room is messy and in shambles. This makes me feel overwhelmed.

Yellow sticky notes fill a wall. Why? Phone messages? I won't be talking on the phone for months. Everyone is heightened and anxious. I need everyone to be calm. This is not helping.

I am very happy to be home. I will cope because I am home. Things are looking up. I can smell the eucalyptus trees, see the sunshine, and recognize sounds. I am home and in my own bed. It feels like a cloud.

Still, I can't sleep. Can't turn my brain off because it seems like all of my life experiences are playing through my head, like my brain is trying to rewire my memory. Stuff I haven't thought about in years. This is exhausting. It feels like a movie reel. But still lots of things I can't remember.

I am pushing out the gory details. Not ready to go there yet.

I AM HOME. THANK YOU.

Haley is tucked into bed. She is having seizures and is on medicine. We don't know what her possibilities are. HOPE is all we have. We love her and that is all that matters.

SEPTEMBER

Changing my bandages takes two hours, twice a day. It helps that my sister is a nurse. She is doing everything for me. She is setting the daily goals because I am too mentally frail to think of anything.

Days fly by doing nothing but lying in bed with my thoughts. I can't eat. I can't keep anything down. Everyone is worried. I told them I was under stress. No kidding. I can still feel the IVs in my arm. I can still hear the machines beeping. It takes me a few seconds after I wake up from a nap to realize that I am at home.

My sister Margie came up with a sleep plan. Sleeping pills never worked for me but Corona did. Viva la Corona!

NEXT DAY

Wow, my hair is growing in a different color. Where has my red hair gone? Very sad. I have bald spots on the back of my head.

Went to see the doctor today and he didn't recognize me. I had clothes on. He was worried I was so thin. I reminded him that I wasn't pregnant and that he had seen me at my worst. This is more like my size. I told him I had had another life before this happened. He told me that my wounds are looking good. I told him that I had not looked. He was shocked. I told him that I didn't want to go into shock looking at them.

I have to protect myself from the reality. I can only handle one piece at a time. It feels like I have let my body down. It was so broken. I have treated it so well all these years, feeding it healthy food and exercising every day. I never took my health or athletic abilities for granted. Even when I was running as a little kid out in the fields by myself or under the cover of darkness in my small town, I knew that running was special. It made me feel happy and strong. Good thing. I need every bit of good health to survive this.

OCTOBER 1

Victory. I am walking around the house holding on to the walls. I seem to have no balance on my right side. Talking more. Can't remember verb tenses at all. I am finally able to sleep.

The movies of my life story are still running through my head. Can't figure out what is real, can't relate to life. Can't cope with what the future will be. Yesterday's gone, yesterday's gone. I feel like I have a secret inside of me and no one will believe it, so I keep it to myself. Need to figure out how I am going to survive and then I will think about what to do for Haley. I need to join the "I Survived Death" club. Where do I sign up?

Tired and foggy. Body is in so much pain.

OCTOBER 10

Margie is leaving soon. My parents arrived. My sister is teaching my mum to change my bandages, a very gruesome task. This is not what my mum is good at, it is my dad. He fed me in the hospital. He cared for his own bedridden mother for years. He wanted to be a doctor.

My bedding has to be changed every day to keep my environment sterile. Margie is teaching Wes how to be the mother. Wes has never been around a baby. He is learning.

Having flashbacks about the accident and the OR. Realizing my life is gone. How do I live? How did I live through that?

Was that death I felt?

OCTOBER 30—SLEPT THROUGH OCTOBER

It still takes Haley two hours to suck two ounces of milk. She usually throws it up. She doesn't sleep, barely breathes. Her whole body is stiff like a board because she doesn't get enough oxygen. She is frightened and is hard for me to hold and manage in my state. Her cries are piercing and haunting. No one is sleeping.

NOVEMBER 1

Looked in the mirror at my body today. Who is this stranger? I've got more scars than a hockey goalie. Thanks goodness I didn't look any sooner. It will be a couple of years before the bruising goes away. Looks like I have 2 belly buttons. I need plastic surgery.

I am trying to rewire my brain because I have an altered reality and I don't remember enough of the past. I am trying to establish some kind of baseline for my personality. I keep wondering when the drugs are going to wear off. I just need some rest. Maybe that will fix me up.

DECEMBER 1 AM

Surf's up. My incisions have closed, so I thought I would try swimming. I swam in the slow lane for the first time in my life and the seniors were blowing by me. It felt great to be weightless. I scared the other ladies in the changing room with my scars.

DECEMBER 1 PM

Taken up Coke and Doritos. Finally I can eat something and not lose it. I never ate like this before. Whose blood did I get? Where did these taste buds come from?

Body is turning yellow, less bruising. Good sign. Broken arm feels good. One point for me. Hoorah!

Put on a bra for the first time and went to the hairdresser. It will be a long time until I can wear pants. They rub up against all the scars and hurt. First time I had to tell someone I knew what had happened. I don't know what words I mumbled, but my friend Margaret from work got the message that something bad had happened. I used to be in Human Resources in this store in the Santa Monica Mall. I need to slip by the people I know. I can't talk, it's too painful. They won't recognize me anyway.

FLASHBACKS

A dead sea of green masks and gowns. The smell of death in the air. No one is talking to me; I was a body they were trying to save. So many people in the room. It's frightening. They are just trying to save us.

My Nephrologist was the Shah of Iran's kidney doctor too. He was so nice. He came into my room and hugged me. The trauma doctor apologized for taking out my uterus. He said he had to do it to save my life. I was hemorrhaging too much. I know it wasn't his fault.

Still can't read. I must be drugged still. No memory. Eyes are crossed. I think I am in trouble. I can't read music either. What has happened? Barely able to do anything.

Everybody looks after Haley. I am too sore and weak to hold her for more than a few minutes. She is so beautiful. I am so sad. This was not the way her life was supposed to be.

DECEMBER

I'm feeling blue. Nothing going on but the rent. I wonder what I am going to be when I grow up?

I need the one minute manager idea. I will just take my life one minute at a time. If I don't look too far in advance, I won't get overwhelmed.

I want to make the best of the minute I am in.

OK, let's trying standing on my own. I need the mirror so I can see what I look like when I stand. A bit crooked. Move to the left a little. That is better. Wow, my calves are jiggling when I move. They look very weird with the muscles hanging down. I think I need them to hold my body up. Let's work on those first.

What am I going to do about this hair that is broken, grey and frizzy? Somebody could fix this.

I need repair. I am now sleeping twelve hours a night with two naps. Need so much sleep. I never put clothes on because I am in bed all the time. I should get out of this moo-moo that my sister bought at the grocery store. I was so bloated and had so many abdominal wounds that I needed something loose to wear.

There is a pile of get-well cards to look at. I wonder if I can read the signatures. Seems overwhelming. My soul feels frail.

DECEMBER 15, MAYBE

I didn't come home with a follow up plan or wellness plan. This makes me feel like there is no help for me. How does this happen? No rehab. My body and brain are damaged. I guess I will have to figure it out myself.

I wrote a grocery list. It took two hours. Spelling is bad. Handwriting is worse. I can think of things in my head, but can barely figure out how to get them written down on paper. I think my intellect is gone. I can't remember how to read, spell, write, do vocabulary or grammar. Nothing, nada, niet, zip. I have been using my finger to guide and try to move from word to word and remember the word I just read. I can't move my eyes to the next line. I feel like I have lost my best friend. Reading was my friend. Who am I without this? This was a big part of me.

My possibilities feel restricted. I will never be able to go to grad school or work again. I have limited comprehension and feel disorganized in my brain. I can't get the right words from my brain to my lips. I am saying stuff that I don't mean to say when I talk. Everything is locked in my mind. I can't walk down stairs. I have no depth perception. I feel so fragile and alone.

DREAMING ABOUT RUNNING

Running was my body's fuel. Running made me tough. I got all my mental toughness from running. It made me feel like I could accomplish anything. It is going to take years to get my body to function. I feel like I have lost my lifeline. My ability to commit to everything flowed out of my ability to commit to running. Losing all my blood destroyed my muscle integrity. I wonder if I will ever get any body strength back.

Watched some guy on TV talking about the warm glow of dying. Really? Death scared the shit out of me! So where do I fit in? What am I to do now that I know how it all goes down?

I need to live my life but it looks like I may be living it from a bed. How am I to live up to having my life saved? I am confused. I am isolated.

I went to a bookstore hoping that there was a book about a young woman killed in a car accident who then survives at the hand of God. I am looking for a real How-To manual that will show me what to do to survive, erase the death memories, let me know that others have been saved at death and, oh yeah, show me what to do with my life. I need to know that everything will be fine at the end of the book.

I will have to get someone to read this book to me. I will just keep looking for it.

DECEMBER STILL

Physically can't muster enough muster to go out. Intellectually vapid. My channels aren't working. I sit in the chair till I go to bed. I watch TV, but don't remember what I watched. Everyone is stressed. They want the miracles to just keep coming. We have used up every free pass.

ANOTHER DAY

Crying all day except when other people are around. I am pretending that I am fine. They have all been through enough. The flood gates are opening up. My heart is broken over Haley. I don't care about myself. I just want Haley to have a life. I wonder if Haley will be alive each morning. She doesn't breathe well, and she can't suck. She is so tense and frightened. I am inadequate for the job at hand.

NEXT DAY

I need a theme song but can't decide between "You're So Vain" or "I Haven't Got Time for the Pain" by Carly Simon. After all,

I have stretch marks on my face from the fifty pounds of fluid retention due to failing kidneys and doctors needing to put all my body fluids back in. My hair is fried and a different color. I am still a whiter shade of pale in the face and black-blue everywhere else. I am going to go with "You're So Vain" because I don't want to talk about the pain.

Hospitals are very humbling. As soon as I arrived in the OR, they cut my clothes off. There I was with my enormous pregnant self for all the world to see. I lost control of my pride right then. Now I could care less if I ever get out of this muumuu. But I do feel sad about my body. I let it down. I couldn't protect it.

I want to move to greener pastures. I want to leave these memories behind.

DECEMBER 25

Cried all the way through church. Gut wrenching sobs, headache producing sobs. Strangers were giving me tissues.

My sports car after being hit head on at 90 mph

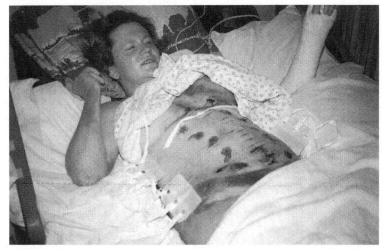

This is what I looked like the day I was sent home from the hospital

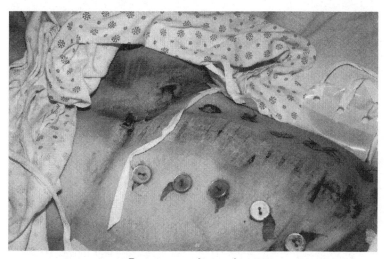

Buttons, staples, and tape

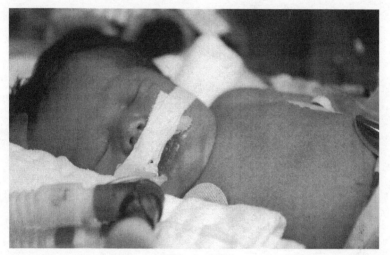

Haley in ICU

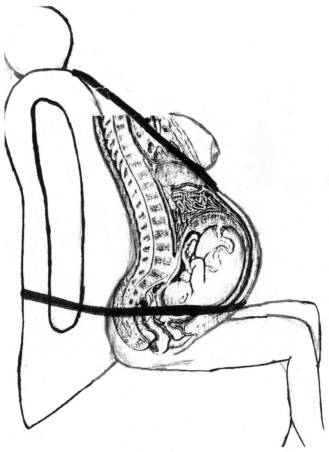

How the seat belt, the force of the crash, and
a full-term baby nearly killed me

BREATHE
...MY STORY, PART II

STRAP IN, IT'S GOING TO BE A ROLLER COASTER RIDE TO RECOVERY

IT'S A NEW YEAR, 1989

Tried to put on some jeans. Too painful, they put pressure on my organs and they began to throb and I got nauseous. Still have to wear extra-large clothes so that nothing puts pressure on my abdomen.

I have gone out of the house a couple of times. I like to go to Manhattan Beach and sit on a bench and watch the waves and people pass by. I am so grateful to be able to get out of the house. The sunshine feels glorious. I would like the sunshine to heal my wounds. This beach is my place. This is where I used to run. I am not sad about this today. This is a victory. I close my eyes and pretend I am running. This is such a long way from the hospital. The wheelchair has given me some freedom.

I went to my regular doctor today for the first time. This is my first outing alone. It felt strange to drive down Main Street, Santa Monica, and see people out doing normal things, like shopping and going to the beach. One day I will be able to do this again. Right now I am worried about parking.

I have to circle the block to get close enough to the doctor's office so that I don't use my energy up walking a couple of blocks. No easy feat when it is so close to downtown Santa Monica. Now I have to remember to feed the meter before I leave the car. Take the money out and hold it in my hand or I will forget to do this. Oh yeah, lock the car too. One more thing: I need to remember where I parked. These are a lot of steps to remember. I have to remember to tell the receptionist that I am here. I forgot to do that at the dentist and had to wait forever.

This is harder than I thought. I wasn't prepared to see all the pregnant women and the women with babies. I might lose it here in the waiting room. I don't know that anyone would know what to do with me. This is a very trendy doctor's office with very trendy people in it. They made a TV series about it. Very LA. I am not feeling or looking very trendy.

My doctor Marki is great. She is a runner and very down to earth. As soon as she walked in I broke down. Talk about lost dreams! She went through my medical records and told me what had happened to my body and things to look out for in the future. She gave me the name of a psychologist, but I know I won't call her. I can't talk about what happened yet. I can't even look at all the broken parts to my life yet. I am afraid that once I start crying I will never stop.

I found my car. Winner! The 405 was bumper to bumper all the way home. It is quite amazing that I am driving. Probably shouldn't be.

JANUARY

I have pretty much mastered walking, at least in my own mind. It only took five months. No more holding on to the wall. I do need to be reminded to stand up straight when I do it. Stairs are still hard. There is something challenging about shifting my weight, lifting my legs and figuring out where the step is. I do not want to fall.

I am going to tackle running soon. I am not going to tell anyone because they will have a bird. I just need to score points for my team. I need it for a grip on reality. I feel so much stress. I need to release it. This is the way I know how to release everything. I need running to begin to build my courage back up. I feel empty and weak. I need the Zen that this will give me. I think if I can recapture this part of my life, I can recapture other parts. I am depending on running to heal me.

JANUARY 9

I snuck out on my own in my running shoes and walked over to the neighborhood running track at the end of the block. I have no idea how to start this running movement, so I watch others. My brain has no memory of how to get started. How do I fly?

I keep watching and watching and thinking and thinking. Then I decided to sort of hop, jump and throw myself forward. Wow, I am moving. It was the take-off that was hard; the moving forward part is easier. Wow, every part of my body feels weak.

But I flew. I know that I can cope with the tomorrows now. Everything feels possible. The healing begins now one step at a time. I can gather momentum now in my life. I have somewhere to take the pain and give it away.

Today I reclaimed one lost dream, on eagle's wings.

FEBRUARY

Running every day, although sometimes it is just in my mind. It is slow and barely resembles a jog. Sometimes I go out twice a day just to keep my mind positive. There is a great park at the end of the block that has this track-type path up high. It is perfect for me right now.

FEBRUARY STILL

Went and ran on the Strand today, no wheelchair. I did not have to watch the other runners. I was one of them. Victory! This is the place for all the hard bodies, whether they are runners, bikers, skaters, or strutters. I also see the hurt, and the recovering athletes. I probably ran past all the hurt people before and never even noticed them. Now I notice. I feel their pain. I want to tell them that there is hope and recovery. It is so good to be back.

What am I running to? Can't shut off my mind. The memories and flashbacks are starting to come. I am beginning to remember every horrifying detail. I feel compelled to remember, but I don't want to because it is so frightening.

Song lyrics, prayers, poetry are playing in my brain and on my lips when I run. It is like these words are becoming a part of my new personality. I never had this happen to me before. These words seem to be new interpretations of life for me. I feel like I am re-wiring my brain and programming in new data. I can't seem to stop this process. It starts each time I run. It seems like I am observing my own life right now as I am being put back together. One thought and one memory at a time. I end each run in tears.

What do I do with these flashbacks? I can't handle them. Thank goodness only little blips come into my mind. If it was the whole movie I would collapse.

I go out each day to the streets and hills of Ladera Heights. The hills have become my challenge. I figure if I can trudge up each hill, it means that I can overcome all the other hills in my life. No matter how slow I go, I refuse to stop. It feels victorious. When I come down the hills the tears of joy come. I can't believe I am able to do this. Good thing that no one is home in these neighborhoods. I must be quite a sight. The gardeners don't seem to care.

I have met some new people who don't know what happened to me. I don't have to explain anything. It gives me some relief. They all think that I am quiet. That is because talking is still so hard; to put thoughts together in the right order and get them out at exactly the right time. I don't think anyone would have described me as quiet before. I don't know if I will ever be that person again.

I think I haven't figured out how to listen and talk at the same time. If the room is noisy I can't make any sense of what people are saying. There is too much disorganization in my brain. When I get this tired I have to lie down and rest in complete silence. My face hurts when I am not able to understand what people are saying. My EverReady is dead. I need to be recharged. It takes a few hours to be able to hear and understand again.

I felt so exposed when I went to the Santa Monica Mall today, like I have a victim sign on my head. Because I have to walk so slow and careful, I think I look like a good target to mug. This is not the way to walk around in LA and be safe. I do better at the grocery store where I can hold onto the cart. I look more normal.

I went back to work today. My career had been a big part of me. I wanted to recapture this. Driving through the Baldwin Hills, up Crenshaw to Wilshire Boulevard felt so unreal to me. I can't believe I am doing this. Trying to walk in high heels was quite a feat, and wobbly. My staff looked at me and I did not know what to say. I went into my office. I really don't have the words for what happened. What can I say? *I died three times and it is so good to be back!* I asked them to remind me to stand up straight. That is all I said about it.

But it was another point scored for my team.

EARLY MARCH

Work is an escape. I don't take any lunch breaks and I occupy my brain with work, trying to stay far away from reality. This is a good break for me. I am glad to be here. The business of the day is a relief from my worries. I talk on the phone and interview all day long. I don't need to talk to anyone about what happened. I just need some distance.

Haley is still not sleeping much. She cries non-stop. She has seizures. Life is unfair for her. I am so happy she is alive, but my heart is broken. Trying to mend and trying to pretend that life is OK.

Worried about all the car-jackings. What if they take Haley? I don't feel safe anywhere. I don't like it when people approach my car and try to wash my windshields. I don't like strangers approaching me. I think that is because I am so physically weak and can't rely on any problem solving skills. I could not kick any-one's butt right now.

I remember the dream....Waking up as I lay dying....

I haven't told anyone about the deaths except my sister Mar-gie. So here I am in a Club of One. I am living with the knowledge of dying. It feels lonely in this club.

Somebody told me today that I could survive this because I am such a strong person. That Haley is lucky we are her parents. All this does is make me feel lonely. The wounded stay behind. Who can help the broken strong people?

I am trying to pretend to be well for everyone else. Anytime I tell someone how bad I feel, they panic. So I quit talking about it. I live in conflict. I am the walking wounded, walking coma. I am in the desert without water. Just keep putting one foot in front of another, keep moving. That is the solution. If can move I can make it through the rest. This will help me build my mental strength. I am afraid if something else major happens I will not be able to cope. My core is void, I feel unprotected and my soul feels exposed.

I have to figure out how to rebuild my inner self.

MARCH

That hill is steep. It does not matter how slow I go, I am going to make it up this hill. I can never stop. I know there is a way. I need to be closer to the top. This is my life line. I need to get to the top of all the hills.

I keep going deeper and deeper into myself to find the courage and strength to go one more round. I will not give up on my health. I don't talk about the pain. There is no point. It won't change anything. I am living it, why talk about it? The pain won't kill me. I know that. But I can't rebuild without some of this pain. I fall into bed at night in such pain. There is no escape. But this is a goal worth achieving. The solutions are somewhere inside of me. I must not let this pain define me. When the pain is enough it will end. I need my competitive edge to beat it. Losing is not an option. I am right smack up against the reality of my life. Only I can figure out how to put light on this darkness. I need a revised life strategy, one with goals and timelines so that I can realistically know that I am moving forward.

When I get to the top of Ladera Heights I can see all the way to Signal Hill in Long Beach. I can see the ocean. What a victory today. I feel closer to heaven up here.

Holding onto hope. There are only two choices here, success or failure. Hope has triumphed over hopelessness for me, so I will keep hoping.

APRIL

Whose blood did I get anyway? The meat cravings are crazy. I can't get enough steak and ribs, a funny diet for a vegetarian. I am even going to All American Burger on Wilshire by myself. It tastes so good.

Thank goodness they didn't pull the plug on me.

I went back to UCLA Medical Center. I was the show part of show and tell medical lecture. I did not go into the lecture hall until the lecture was over. I couldn't listen to them talk about my "blunt force trauma." They wrote about me in a medical journal as well. Very surreal.

I asked that no one ask me any questions. I have not found my voice. I can't put vocals to my story yet. How do I tell people what really happened? Should I stay or should I go…whose song is that? I don't want all the attention. But I want to thank people for helping me.

When I walked in everyone stood up and clapped. I was overwhelmed. There were a few hundred people in the room. I wanted to thank them but I had no voice. Many people came up to me and told me they had been on my case. I thanked them. A million thanks. Overwhelmed with emotion.

I walked the halls of UCLA Med Center in disguise. Nobody knew it was me. People did not come over to touch me or talk to me. I can't tell them it is me. This still feel like a war zone. I am afraid to look anyone in the eyes in case they recognize me. I can't talk. I used to close my eyes when they wheeled me down the corridors. I couldn't look at the expressions of people watching me. *Dead mother walking.* I just retreated into myself. I couldn't deal with the reality of how many people kept me alive. I know they were so happy I survived, but I did not know what to do with all the emotions I had. I had so many hospital workers stopping in to see me when I got out of the coma. They would come in and tell me that they did such and such on my case, or their friend was there in the OR, or they flew MedStar and wanted to meet me because they had heard about me. Finally they had to put a "No Hospital Staff Visitation" sign on my door. I was not getting any rest in between dialysis and bandage changes and med rounds and my family. I still did not sleep.

People kept asking me if I was going to write a book. Hello? I just died a minute ago.

Need a "How To" Manual on Surviving

I am going to figure out who I am.

I just need this to get through this survival period first. I need to know for sure that I am going to survive. I know that what happens from here is up to me. The problem is that I am not the same person who got wheeled into the ER. I don't know who this new person is. The circumstances I am in are not going to change, but I need to change how I am going to think about them. Otherwise I will be that poor woman with that sad story. I need a different identity.

I need a map, a guide on how to lead myself to the next stage of life. I want to feel whole on the inside, outside and upside downside. I know there is light at the end of the tunnel; I have been there before. I saw that light at the end of the coma tunnel. I want to live successfully again. I want to regain me and a better me.

I know what this means. I am going to have to remember it all so that I can move on from there. Yuck.

RUNNING, TRYING TO CATCH MY SPIRIT.

Work is feeling pointless.

Living with the knowledge of death changes you.

SOME MAY DAY

Grocery shopping is ridiculous. It takes forever. I am so exhausted after. It is a very multi-tasking activity. It is hard to read the list, then look for it on the shelf and then check the list to make sure I got the right thing. There is no way I can add coupons to this process. I have tried. I can't read the coupon and then find the item and get the size right and the expiration date and on and on. But it is my only outing. At least I have found some food I like again. Each week I try something new. A lot of food doesn't taste good to me. Is that the drugs?

ANOTHER MAY DAY

Stayed in bed all day, can't stand straight. Well, the truth is, I spend a lot of time in bed. Mostly I am always in bed. I just get out of bed to do a few things and then I have to go back to bed to rest after that. I am making it sound like I am back living life. Not yet. Soon.

Right now my life is lying down because I am too hurt to sit.

But I am so much better off than I have been. I am thinking about running in the mountain meadow today. Segment the pain. Put it somewhere separate in my brain. Don't allow it to take over my whole brain. Just feel the pain where the pain is. Don't let it be felt everywhere. My prayer is to take it out of my mind.

I feel out of balance and off balance. I feel stuck in this life of pain and fog. Flashbacks are coming more and more. It is so draining. I am crying all day. Mourning loss. It is draining my spirit. I have got to visit all of the sorrow, experience all of it. Bring it to the light so I can make sense of what happened to me in the hospital.

Was I supposed to die? Did destiny come and I eluded it? Am I not supposed to be here? Did I do something wrong and mess up God's plan? I need to understand why I got to live. What is the purpose of my being allowed to live? I feel so burdened by this.

I will let all the sorrow for Haley ooze out of my wounds. Somewhere inside of the pain and sorrow is the answers.

This is going to get ugly. But if I don't go there, I will not being living a life of truth.

I get it. I get the pain. I need to choose what kind of pain I want—the pain of staying where I am at or the pain of moving through it. I think the pain of staying stuck in this place is worse. I need to be courageous to press through all of this. I need to meet this problem that has got be backed up against the wall with an even greater force in order to push it away from me.

It may have to hurt even more in order to feel better one day. I think that goal is worth all the pain it is going to take to get there. That is it. I really hate this place I am in. I want a better life. I want it really bad. I am going to start moving through all of this physical and emotional pain. The effort will be worth it. I trust that there is a better life and that if I keep faith and hope next to me, I can find it.

NEW DAY, SOME MONTH, ONE DAY AT A TIME.

I am at a fork in the road again. Where do I begin?

Let's start with the goal of feeling better. My bones are poking through my clothes and I have no strength to sit up. But I haven't thrown up in a month. I think my body can start to process more food. I know I can't get strong without good food. Thank goodness I have been on vitamins and know how important these are to rebuilding my body. I always ate healthy, so I don't have to wean myself off junk food. I just have to wean my stomach onto more food and keep it down. Stress has removed my appetite completely. I guess I need to eat whether I feel hungry or not. I know that I can't rebuild muscle mass without protein. My first dream is to reclaim a healthy body.

I know that part of my healing is going to involve mourning all of my losses and letting my past dreams go. Otherwise I am holding onto all of the things that are not real. I am living in broken dreams, not new dreams. I am going to have to face all the dreams I had for Haley never coming to be. Her losses are irreplaceable. I feel like retching.

BREATHE. JUST BREATHE.

One more step, run around the corner up the last part of the hill and see the ocean. Don't forget to **breathe.** Get a grip, quiet the soul, shut off the noise of the world, and feel God's graces flowing through me. Don't get tense, relax.

Tension holds me back. Trying harder doesn't work. Find the ease, find the pace, find my inner calm, energize and then accelerate and excel. Get into the zone. Feel the miracle of my life. Soak up the healing sunshine and sweat out the poison. Repair, rebuild and renew my mind, body and spirit. Soar above the turmoil, soar above the ground and go for higher goals.

Gratitude. Thank you for my life.

JUNE

I need every cell in its best state to repair this wounded body. I have great respect for my body and all it has been through. Vitamins, minerals, water, oxygen, veggies, protein, exercise, rest, and sleep. I attack my wellness plan with the same passion I have used to accomplish all my previous goals in my BA—Before Accident life. I didn't eat junk food before so I better get rid of the diet cokes and Doritos.

I am good at being consistent, so I need to make a plan my body can rely on again. I don't want to still be lying in bed year after year. I need to start building up my muscles again. I need strength. I know my body and athletics and fitness. I can figure out a plan for myself. I will start with one body part at a time. If you do not have your health, it is hard to have anything else. This needs to be first on my rebuild list: WELLNESS. I want to still be here next year and the year after that. I will not quit.

I have no room in my plan for toxins. I got enough of that with all the drugs they gave me in the hospital. I have opted for no pain killers at all. Seems nuts, but they could have become an entire problem on their own. I also thought that if I couldn't feel where it hurt, how would I know what to focus on when praying and meditating on good health? I know that my system is screwed up. I can feel it. I can look at my hair, skin color, and eyes and see that all systems are not functioning yet. I know I am out of balance.

I need to be kind to my body. It is to be respected and nurtured. I have got to get back to the wellness I had before I got hurt.

JULY

I need a hobby. I used to read, but what can I do now? I don't remember how to play the piano. The only sport I can do is walk and sort of run. I need suggestions.

I gave away all my suits for work today. I need to stay home and fix Haley. She is cortically blind, can't move any limbs, has overly sensitive hearing and is barely breathing.

I have put all my friends into support roles. I don't want to burn any of them out. One I live vicariously through, one I tell all the real parts of the story to, and another asks me about Haley. And I have a new friend who does not know anything. I am trying to open the window to my world and see what comes in.

I have started working on reading. I am working at it one word at a time. I now know what the word is and what it means, but I can't string them into a sentence and understand the sentence. That will be next. There is such a great need for me to be able to read. I need to understand what is wrong with Haley and me in order to fix the problems.

STILL JULY

I see them when I am out in public, the walking wounded. It might be a limp, a protected way of walking or eyes diverted, but I can see their pain. My body aches when I see their bodies ache. I don't want anyone to feel like I do.

I am so sad when I see it in children. I wish I could take all the suffering from Haley and bear it myself. I can do this, but she is too little for all of the pain. It is her pain that doubles me over.

Not fair.

I ask God to take my life and give it to her. It does not look like that is His plan for me. I need to get stronger so I can do more for her. I need to be able to lift her and feed her and take her out of the house. She needs a life too. This matters for her. I tie her onto my body so I can help her breathe. She sleeps next to me at night so that I know she is alive. She is knocking on heaven's door.

SEPTEMBER

Tried riding a bike today but I couldn't stay on the bike. I have no balance. Seems like everything I do, I have to relearn. I needed to recover from those few blocks. Using my muscles differently hurts.

How about "Staying Alive" by the Bee Gees? Maybe that should be my theme song.

Went to Neiman Marcus in Beverly Hills to meet a friend for lunch. What an outer body experience that was. I am not relating to this world anymore. I can't even explain how odd it felt to walk around the store. Retail was my work world before I went into recruiting. It is like pageantry. Now it feels strange and disconnected.

SEPTEMBER, LATER

I need to get out of this bed or I am going to rot. I need more sunlight. I need to make a plan for each day so that I can break through the pain barriers each morning and get myself up and out of bed. The mornings are hard because the tasks are daunting. I am going to write a plan for each day. This will give me motivation.

Thank goodness for my friend Margaret. She understands as she has had the jump starts as well. She knows the big secrets of life and death. I can tell her how bad it is and she has been there. She knows it is just the truth. She calls me a lot of mornings while I am still in bed and she coaxes me out. We talk about a lot of things for a long time. Real life things. It helps to know someone who has been to hell and back and is choosing to live life. There is one other person in the Club.

What was it that put me at the top of my game before? Sucks that I can't remember who I was before. I am sort of pretending to be myself. But I am not fooling myself. I keeping running and thinking about who I am. How did I survive those days in the hospital? I keep dissecting and analyzing it, trying to find myself in it. What are the daily practices that I had before that I need to implement to get myself back and win this game? I was very diligent and focused when I wanted to achieve something. I can feel that inside of me. Put what exactly did I do and how did I do this?

I am running the best I can. When I am not running, I am praying or talking to myself. I am trying to only keep positive thoughts in my head. The conversations I have in my head while I run never stop. I go home right after and write down my thoughts, the memories and experience of this ordeal. I must take them out of my head and safeguard them somewhere. This is helping me cope and be sane. Writing helps me sort through all of my emotions.

I am building a calendar with timelines for when I need to accomplish milestones. I am writing new strategies on how to live this new life. I am trying to create a new picture of what my life can be about. This way I can figure out what direction I am supposed to go in next.

I really am visualizing my life. These visions are becoming my dreams. This is giving me something to work toward. I keep these visions in my mind and hope that they will become my reality. These visions need to be attainable and possible. I need them to be true. I can't live in a fantasy. I need to face reality.

This journal is helping me. It is my true thoughts about my life and how I have experienced this chapter. This is not anyone else's interpretation of this event. This is not how others are hoping that I am coping. This journal is helping me save my life.

ANOTHER DAY

Hard to write today. Right arm is full of nerve pain from the pinched nerves in my neck. I am trying to write lying down propped on pillows. Can't move the arm at all. Searing pain. Not coping well with this pain level. I am jumpy and agitated. My friends can hear the pain in my voice and keep asking me if I am OK. I am pacing in pain but I am not stopping.

This has been going on for a long time. I have come to realize that the pain of stopping all of my dreams would be worse than this pain. I need to write. Why is this happening now?

Why in my weakest moments has the scourge of worry become a part of me? I was a positive thinker before. It hardly seems fair to have worry on my mind. I need to focus on hope to counterbalance this. If I feel worried, I am not going to let it stop me. I'll do it worried. So what? I am doing it.

I am running with my right arm down by my side. Praying for healing. Feeling the pain but I am not going to give up and quit anything. I would just be lying in bed with the same pain and accomplishing nothing. At least this way I got a positive good run in that left me empowered.

Why is this barrier coming up now? Why is it trying to stifle my voice?

I must go back to the journey; the answers are in the journey. What does this even mean?

EVERY DAY

Found the remote control for the TV in the fridge. Short term memory sucks. There is no pattern to the memory loss. Sometimes I can remember what I just did and other times I can't. Short term memory is causing some problems. I can't pay bills correctly, or do any paperwork. I make so many mistakes. Very challenging.

I am realizing that I have some brain injuries from the car accident. I thought it was all of the drugs and if I got them out of my system, then I would be able to think clearer. Looks like the brain gets hurt when you stop breathing so many times!

I really need to program my brain with some new data. I am like a revisionist. I can rewrite my own story. But the truth is I don't know what all the pieces from the past are so I guess I am really creating my own backstory and storyline.

More poetry, song lyrics, and smart remarks are circling around in my head. I usually ponder these to see what they mean to me. These are all good positive thoughts in my head, even the funny sarcastic ones. I need to put new thoughts into my head so that they can overtake the flashbacks.

1990

Wish my midlife crisis looked like a Porsche and gold chains.

I miss my work identity. I have no role models for this life. I feel peerless. I am walking down the road less traveled. I know this road. I have had many forks in the road of my life. I always chose the one less traveled. Commitment and determination will help get me through. Faith and hope will get me through. You have got to believe in something or none of this makes any sense.

The meat just keeps coming. I can't get enough meat. I am just craving protein and iron and water. And I am rebuilding. I need so much iron I could eat metal. I am always starving.

My workouts are starting to look like workouts. I have started to weight train. Three pound weights are a start. I have to take a few days off in between my workout days to see how all the parts feel and check if I tore any muscles. After rest and recovery I go back to it. At least I know that when I hurt now it will help me in the end. If I don't start with these little weights I won't get stronger.

I am working out at a small body builder gym on Venice Boulevard. It seems like the right place for me. I don't know what the body builders think. But I am building and bulking up too!

I am doing Haley's therapy all day long. She deserves a gold medal. She is a miracle. She is what faith and hope look like. Wes and I fill her day with love and opportunities to soar. I fill my day with her purpose. I must help her fulfill her purpose in life. Her life depends on me never quitting. I can't choke. If I choke, she dies. I have to know that I have given her my best. Others are depending on me getting to the finish line.

Haley is an example of being the best that you can be and never complaining or giving up. Her soul is strong and I am pulling strength from her and her purpose. I think the purpose of this journey is attached to Haley's journey. I am starting to see glimmers of purpose in this tragedy. This is good. This is a good day. I must discover what can be good in all of this.

I dream at night about Haley walking. Others are having this dream. Her journey is hard. She has to fight for every breath. She has attracted some wonderful people in her life that care about her and they come to our house to help us do therapy with her. Many of her volunteers are complete strangers, lifting her out of her cage on eagle's wings. She is flourishing because of this love and acceptance.

They support me because they are helping Haley. They did not know me before, so they think I am the quiet type. I listen to them talk and escape into their lives to have a break from mine. It really helps me to be around these well people. This is who I want to be like: well, healthy people with a life.

It's not a life when you can't get out of the house very often. I hope one day I can stand as an example of survival. I hope that I can survive and rebuild. I think I can. But the true measure is where I am ten and twenty years down the line.

I have seen one of Haley's neurologists from UCLA on a TV talk show. He is not very supportive of parents taking alternative therapeutic paths to help their kids. He pretty much drugs them and writes them off. He was talking about one of his patient's parents who sought out other means of improving their brain injured son's life and they have seen vast improvement in him. They made a movie out of this. The doctor knew he was depicted in the movie as not so supportive.

Got to love LA. People know how to get things done and spread the word. And then they make a movie. It is very inspiring.

I am grateful we found the Institutes in Philadelphia to help us with Haley. It looks like they are a match with us. Against all odds they believe that Haley can make progress.

Here is one of those forks in the road, and we chose the road less traveled. We are determined that Haley will make improvements and not be stuck in the same place forever. Hope suits us. There was not one moment of hesitation in deciding that this was the path for Haley. There is a great sense of conviction in the room.

Another step in our new life plan, another dream to be mended. I will stay with this first step until I know what to do next.

I am reading a little bit now. I know what the sentence says. It is probably a seven-year-old reading level. This is a victory. I understand it at the time, but can't remember what I read. Painfully frustrating.

I never really tell anyone that I can't read.

1991

The year is flying by. Haley's therapy is all consuming. I am back in my one minute manager mode. All the problems to fix are so overwhelming that I am better if I just look at the day, one minute at a time. Live in the moment. Make the best out of the present. Don't look to the future right now or it will seem daunting. I am shifting my perception of the problem at hand.

I need to view all of this work to be done as a journey of discovery.

This is another chapter in this story of recovery. Each day is so repetitive. There is no time for creativity. I am just following along with this program. The Institutes have given me a how-to manual on how to improve Haley's abilities. I think I am doing well with all of this. There is no sitting on the sidelines. We are fully in the game.

Her vision therapy takes four hours a day in a dark room with a bright flashlight. I flash the light for one second on and five seconds off. We are trying to stimulate the vision pathway to make it carry the signal from the eye to the brain and back. The good thing is that I can lay down for this activity because I am so exhausted from the 1000 trips Haley makes down the incline plane. We are trying to get her to understand what movement feels like. I have to pick her up at the bottom of the incline plane, carry her to the top, bend over and put her down. So for me, it is 2000 times I am bending over and lifting. Very brutal on my broken body.

But I want this for Haley more than I mind the pain that I am in.

She can move one of her big toes. That is how she pushes herself down. That is such a victory. We are jubilant. She can move!

I am learning to shut all the distractions of the world to reach this deep into *commitment*.

Need to shut out the noise and temptations of the world. I need to focus, listen and work. No time to waste. Time is Haley's enemy. I watch the clock all day to make sure I don't let time slip by. I have to do this while she is young and her brain is young. Fourteen hours a day, seven days a week. Unreasonable situations require unreasonable effort. There is nothing normal about what has happened or what I must do. She deserves our best efforts. I have faith that she will live. On eagles' wings, Haley soars.

1992

Every day is the same, with the same goals. The weeks go by and now the years are going by. I try to only look at one day at a time. The problems will not go away by themselves. I just work through them. I reach for the upper limits of my abilities to do my best for Haley. I follow my own routine of working with her, resting, exercising and sleeping. Then I get up the next day and do it all again. This is my strategy for wellness. When I am fatigued, everything starts to hurt even more. Then I can't push anymore so I stay in bed until I have reenergized. This has become the way I stay balanced. A bit skewed, but this is my reality.

I had a vision in the hospital while I lay dying that Haley would walk.

I feel like I'm fighting a war. Brain injury is a battle.

The barriers of my broken body make it difficult to achieve my goals for Haley. But I rewrite my strategy and I keep moving forward. Doing nothing and letting Haley sit there would be worse. I am working on a solution.

The future is ours to see, so hold on.....Is that Eddie Money in my head?

My friends and their friends keep coming every day to our house to help Haley. We have thirty-six volunteers. They are from Mexico, Sweden, India, Bosnia, China, and all over the US and of course LA.

My house is like LA; people from all over the world come here to work. LA has been so good to us. We have found so many generous people that want to help her. We have as many men as we do women volunteers. Haley knows as much about architecture as she does about cooking ethnic foods, fashion and retail. It is such a wonderful group of people. They have become the high points of my day. They are the only people I see or interact with. They are helping me heal through their generosity of spirit and time. They are taking time away from their lives and families to help us.

What extraordinary examples of compassion. They are helping to raise a family up out of the rubble.

They don't ask much about the details of what has happened; they focus on the rebuilding of our lives. They are such a wonderful distraction from my day to day life. They are the glue that holds me together most weeks. I probably should brush my hair for them.

I am so lucky to know these angels on earth.

With a little help from my friends we can work this all out together.

APRIL

My phone keeps ringing. My friends are all calling to see what I know. They know I am at home watching the news and they are at work, isolated. LA is breaking out into riots and fires. The National Guard just blockaded our road. We live next to a grocery store. Grocery stores are being looted. I can't even go out and get any food. My neighbor brought some of her food over. Wes is coming home from work. We are trying to decide if we need to leave. We are only a few miles from all of the problems. My friends told me that they are all scared. Nobody knows what to do. It feels like anarchy.

It has been many days since we have left our home. I am going to go to the grocery store at six-thirty in the morning tomorrow. It should be safer first thing in the morning.

NEXT DAY

The parking lot is packed. I see a woman about my age, drive up to her and carefully ask her, so that I don't scare her, if I can follow her to her parking stall and also use her grocery cart. I can't shop if I don't have a parking spot or a cart.

I go into the store and it is packed, so packed that I can't get down the aisles of the store. With all the grocery stores that have been looted and burned, people from these areas need to come to Culver City to shop. I park my cart at the end of the aisle, run down it and grab food. The shelves are bare of almost everything.

I see that the lines to check out are extended to the back of the store. I figure the lines in the middle must be short because there is no way to get to those. I make my way through the crowd to find the shorter, jammed-in middle lanes.

I am out of there in less than an hour. My survival skills have come through again. *I am woman, hear me roar.* I can hear Helen Reddy's song in my head. It feels like my brain is 75% song lyrics now.

OCTOBER 1992

I feel like a butterfly in a cocoon. Sheltered, protected, dormant, gathering strength and waiting for a rebirth. I wonder how long this stage will last. It is not time to come out yet. I need to walk the path I am on, listen and wait. I know I am going to want to fly again.

Structure is keeping me focused and I am able to accomplish many goals each day.

I write my goals down and the steps I need to take to accomplish them. I always keep my long term goals in mind. I need to put all the building blocks into place, so one day I will have a foundation on which to build my life again. I take each victory, enjoy it and then move on to the next goal. I use those small victories to give me energy for the next goal. I have a plan; I see my goals in my dreams. I will keep working on Haley and myself each day.

Quitting is never an option.

Sometimes I am afraid that if I ever go out of these walls, I will never come back in. It is very isolating and confining, but I cling to hope. Hope that one day I will see that all the effort was worth it. Hope, please carry me forward.

The daily work is a place for me to take my pain. I am choosing to believe in the journey. I know that I am so far away from where I was. I believe the answers for me are in this journey. I don't know what they are, but I only have this one option open to me.

I will keep putting one foot in front of the other, one goal in front of the other. I am caught somewhere in the middle of this drama.

MARCH 1993

Some days I hit the wall earlier than other days. This is a marathon. Lifting, holding, feeding, cooking, bending, twisting, worrying, breathing, running, resting, and sleeping. Anything worth getting is worth working hard for. The price to overcoming is exhaustion. But exhaustion means that I am working as hard as I can. I know one day things will be different. It is difficult to make the right decisions under these circumstances. I try to be careful and diligent when I make new decisions.

Sometimes I mess up. Sometimes I am afraid to make a decision because I know my brain is not thinking right. But I am aware of all of this and try very hard to think things through and then move forward. These are some of the prices of progress. I am the only one that can fix my problems. I need to push these problems back with more force than they are pushing against me.

I am starting to understand. When I am having hard time physically or mentally it is the force pushing against me.

It is the accident and all the negative things pushing against me trying to make me stop. I am getting refuelled and more energized and I am starting to push back.

I win more often when I move away from worry, fear, frustration, discouragement, exhaustion and depression and on and on. I push back with good thoughts, action, belief, faith, hope, reading, exercise and Haley's therapy. I see what the force is that I need to exert. It is a lot of force. That car hit my dreams at 90 mph. I need a lot of good things surrounding my life and thoughts to create more force than that to push back with.

Someone asked me if I have Haley hooked up to a breathing monitor. I said yes, she is hooked up to me. I sleep every night with my hand on her chest and my ear next to her mouth. I know the second she skips a breath or stops. I never really sleep.

I have been worrying about dying again. I don't want to think about it, but I know why.

I feel worried, I feel vulnerable, I feel weak. I can't face another trauma. I am not renewed yet. I will not have the will to hang in there if something is wrong. I am waiting to hear the results of my blood test. I lost all of my blood. I had my entire system pumped with other people's blood. AIDS has just been identified in 1988 and testing is not mandatory. What are my odds?

Praise the Lord; I am AIDS/HIV free. It must have helped that I was at UCLA and that I have a rare blood type. I used to always get invitations to donate.

Thank God my blood is clean. This is another miracle. This is a heavy blanket of fear that was lifted today.

I should get alumni status at UCLA. I have been given an honorary degree of Living. I pushed back when I went and took that test. Victory! Worry squashed.

A woman asked me today what I did for a living. I was mute. I had no voice. I can't put words to what I do and why I do it.

Many days I have to take Advil and wait an hour before I get up so I can move. My bruised, battered body hurts all day long.

But I do the work anyway. I do wish I had another life. I see others living my life. It makes me sad. My life is working on Haley, myself, running, praying, resting, sleeping and grocery shopping once a month.

I feel the breath of temptation so close to me, telling me to give up.

I am reading *People* magazine now. This is a victory. I can spell some words that I have reprogrammed into my brain. I am still not good with plurals and verb tenses, or prepositions. Still can't read music at all. Can't remember the multiplication table. Working on addition. I write in my journal, but I think only I can understand the spelling. I have to write lying down because I can't bend my head down to look at the paper. I can write standing up at a counter. My arm is in constant pain. But I have to get all these thoughts out of my head and safeguard them on paper. I don't think it is healthy to have all this swirling around inside. I am obsessed with writing stuff down. Maybe scribbling is a better definition than writing.

Haley can see now. She can speak when her breathing is good, which is not very often. She is moving more limbs and gaining weight. She can point and raise her arm when I ask her questions. She understands us and is doing well in her homeschooling. It has been a lot of work to get to this point. The program she is on is working for her. It is such a blessing that we found this therapy. Haley works so hard and is so patient. We love her so much. It is hard work for all of us, but it is worth the effort and sacrifice. We are scoring more points for our team.

I am putting all my hope into this journey. Trusting, believing and praying for a better life for all of us. Nothing has ever taken my hope away. It is strong. I believe my journey with Haley will lead me to a greater understanding of the path I am on. I don't know where my journey is leading but I am learning a lot of things about life, myself and others on the way.

We go to Philly twice a year for Haley to see her support team. It is a pilgrimage of hope. We get all the information we need to go home and put in another six months of hard work with her. The trips are killer on my neck and back injuries. It is hard for my brain to grasp and retain all the important information they give us. Good thing Wes is there. He is my backup brain. It takes me a week in bed to recover from these trips. But it is all worth the pain and effort.

SOMEDAY

I just do and do and do.

Had a spine x-ray. Only three "S" curves in my spine and all my neck vertebrae are jammed together and have completely moved to the right. Oh, and my pelvis is twisted.

I need to pull the covers up. I don't have a plan.

SEPTEMBER 1993

May Day, May Day. I am in crisis. I am not making it. I am being swallowed up by sorrow. I dry my tears only when others are coming to my house. I have headaches all day from crying and crying. I wake up crying in the night. I try to not let Haley know I am crying all day.

Please deliver us from this pain. This is not her fault. It is not her fault that I am falling off the cliff. My brain hurts, my body is in so much pain. I have no life. I have no dreams, I have no abilities. My heart is broken. Life has let me down. The responsibility of surviving is weighing me down. It is too heavy. I can't eat. I can't sleep. I can't fix this. My good is not good enough. The death nightmares have returned. Everyone else lives and I die a slow contorted death.

Raise me up on eagles' wings, please, now. God help me.

Where and how I spent 12 hours a day for 14 years

Myself, Haley, and Wes
Haley is 4 years old, and I am exhausted
from doing all of her therapy

BREATHE

...MY STORY, PART III

PIECING BROKEN DREAMS INTO A LIFE PUZZLE

NOVEMBER 1993

Strategy Time: I am taking up my sword to do battle. I am going to conquer and push back with all my force. Where is my breast plate of armour?

Up at six a.m. before the worry thoughts start. Running and praying and meditating and planning. I am going to work at keeping all the sorrowful thoughts out of my head. Stay busy all day long. I can read a little better. I read, talk to myself, talk to God, pray, talk to friends, talk to Haley, talk to family. Keep my brain completely occupied, so nothing negative gets into it. I pray for faith and guidance. I problem solve and talk and yell and argue when I run.

My best thoughts come when I run. Solutions start popping into my head. I see what it is that I want, and I hold onto it until I figure out how to get it. Through my thoughts, actions and mental talks, I create the day I want. I work joyfully on Haley's program. I stop and work on myself. I stop and rest and relax. I am starting to put some balance into my day. Look how far I have come. I should be able to go farther. I am using my will to live and putting it into these middle years. I have the will to struggle through this rebuilding.

I want it all back. This is not good enough. I want a life. I am going to talk and pray myself back to happy. I am going to listen to joyful music and see the sunshine as a sign that I am going to be renewed. I am going to read more and talk more. I am going to practice all of these things and believe that I will get better at them. I am giving all this sorrow away. Enough! I have had enough.

Cleanse my soul and put my feet on the ground to move forward. Look out, I am taking names. I am moving forward.

This accident is a part of me and will never go away. This journey will be in my life forever. But it is not going to define me. I am not going to be the poor woman with the sad story. The scars are going to remind me that I am alive. The pain is going to remind me that I am breaking through barriers.

Segment the pain. Put the pain somewhere else. It is irrelevant. If it is not going to go away then I will have to put it in its own box and take it with me. I am putting my life into action. There will be bruises and scrapes and a lot of mistakes. But I am not going to sit here and take this life I have been dealt. No way. I don't care that I have not gotten all of my abilities back. I am happy with what I have recovered. It is good enough. I am moving forward. But I am not staying behind because of it.

I am going to dream up some plans. They will be even bigger than before because I can handle it. Look what I can bear. I can bear more than I could before. Look out. I am going to find my voice. I am going to mend my broken dreams.

January 17, 1994

Bang!

Usually I open one eye to see if I actually have to get up. This one sends me flying out of bed and in motion to get to Haley who is sleeping in her respiratory machine. But I can't stand. I have socks on and is the floor is shaking so much I can't stand up. Cripes. I have to crawl to Haley's room.

Ten seconds, twelve seconds; it is still shaking. I can't get the clips undone on her machine because it is shaking so much. I will grab her and bring the machine with me. This earthquake is unbelievable. Must get outside in case the roof collapses.

It's over. Calm.

Is it really over?

We survived the Northridge Earthquake with minimal damage to our house. Many people were not so fortunate.

We went to see the play *I Want to Tell You My Story* by Cornelia MacDonald. She was Haley's nurse in NICU. She helped keep her alive. I am forever grateful. She wrote a play about her life as a poor sharecropper's daughter and the abuse of her childhood. She has written this one-woman play to help heal the wounds of her past. I have seen her play fourteen times. She tells her story from her soul. She is one of the angels on earth. Corny has changed her story. She inspires me.

Overcome and write your story. Tell your story and heal others. Triumph over hardships.

I can feel it. I just didn't know its name. Fortitude, it is fortitude that I have.

I use fortitude every day, month after month after year after year. No gain without fortitude. The fork in the road has been the harder road, the road less traveled. But the lessons have been down this road.

I get it that the purpose was in the journey. I needed to discover what I was really made of. *Fortitude* helps me work on Haley's endless therapy day after day. Fortitude helps me to rebuild my body every day.

Thank you for the gift of fortitude. I wouldn't have made it and gone down this road without it. I have learned all of my life lessons and the meaning of life down this road.

I will learn to read better. I am going to need this. I will start practicing bigger vocabulary. I need to be able to communicate.

I have things to say. When will my voice return? When will I have the courage to speak?

I capitalize on the good and let the bad days go by without comment. I only see the goal at the end of the day, the middle is irrelevant. I stay in my purposeful steps in the middle and take my mind off it. I just do it and quit thinking about it. Mind, body and purpose are in total harmony.

I need fewer days off. I am able to recover and move through the busy days with more ease. I know what I want and where I must go to get it. My pain and sorrow are subsiding. My optimism is growing. I feel more at peace working with purpose. I know what it is that is important in this journey. I will be proof that you never quit, no matter what. Keep on keeping on. There will be something more at the end of this chapter. I can build on these feelings now. The darkness is turning to light. Hope is pulling me through. I am remembering more of who I was. I feel my spirit nearby; deliver me to my purpose.

With Haley tucked away in her respiratory machine for the night, I unwind in my bedroom. I can watch TV or read. I don't just collapse into some kind of half sleep. I am trying to find more moments of gentleness. I am looking for balance against the hard driving beat of my dreams.

EVERY DAY IS A CHOICE. EACH DAY IS A FORK IN THE ROAD.

I can choose to waste the day, or I can choose to fill it with things that will help Haley and me renew and build our lives. Each day I am writing another line in my story. I must create more chapters the way I want them to read. When a barrier comes up, I can dynamite it.

Sometimes I can only crawl. I am constantly pulling and ripping my back and shoulder muscles. Fortitude, I am calling you. Pain is inevitable, whining is optional. Thank goodness for the Blues.

My smart remarks are returning. Oh, that's helpful.

I am making a point of dressing up, putting on makeup whenever I leave the house. I am doing everything to be positive, act positive and do positive things. It does make a difference. What a treat to get out of my sweats and go to the grocery store. I always dress Haley cute when we go out. She deserves to look cute.

One of our dear friends and faithful volunteers died today. His heart was broken over the war in Bosnia. He threw himself into traffic. I can't believe this. We spent so many hours with him. He loved coming to our house and helping Haley. He came for Christmas, the Fourth of July and all the Thanksgivings. He was a part of the family we created in LA. He was so nice, funny and smart. We learned so much about Yugoslavia...Bosnia, Croatia, Serbia. He was knowledgeable about European history.

When the war broke out he couldn't believe it. He grew up in Sarajevo, and told us how civilized everything and everybody was. His parents and one brother were still there and he was trying to help them evacuate. He could hear gunfire when he called and checked up on them. He finally got them out, but he didn't survive the war.

His funeral today was gut-wrenching sad. Everyone was crying. All his work friends were there from UCLA and all his Bosnian friends were there. All of his girlfriends were there from all over the world. He would have liked that. He always said "so many beautiful women, so little time." And then he would laugh that wonderful little laugh. I will remember him always.

Back to UCLA Emergency. I have hairline fractures in my jaw that have gotten infected and my entire head is swollen. One eye is swollen shut. I am reacting to the penicillin. I told them that I feel like I have hives on my brain and in one second they jammed a needle into my back end to stop the swelling.

Very scary. Enough already.

Three root canals later and weeks of pain, I am fixed. Glad all my dentists and specialists were so excellent. It took three of them to solve this problem. They all teach at UCLA Dentistry School as well. I really should have alumni status. Apparently I need UCLA to keep me going.

I think I need to just lay on the beach in Malibu today. That will be cathartic.

The PCH is quiet today. I think about my wild ride down this road on August 21, 1988, every time we drive to Malibu or the Pacific Palisades. Zuma Beach is quiet today. It is peaceful and renewing. I always spent my time at the ocean, riding my bike on the paths that run through the beaches. I never understood how people just laid on the sand and did nothing or only read a book. Seemed pretty boring. Now I understand. It is a way to renew mind, body, and spirit. I am going to plan for more times for renewal and restoration. It is impossible to do ones best when you are weary. I am going to make plans to renew my strength and spirit. I can be creative.

I now know that balance is crucial to succeeding. The temptation to work all the time is a bad temptation. Eventually you are not as effective as when you are renewed.

OK, so there is no way I am stopping running while the chiropractor tries to fix me. Running saved my life and is where I renew my soul. My body knows how to respond to this. If I am not mentally strong, I can't heal.

I am not listening to this prognosis. I have overcome greater things. I believe that this can be fixed. Massage, rest, good nutrition, adjustments, exercise and then start all over again. I need to dial down some of the lifting. It is breaking me down. I need to increase the amount of time I spend on my wellness plan. I have let Haley's program dominate all of my time. It is showing in my body. I am not any good to anyone if I have to go back to bed. Chiro told me I could end up in a wheelchair. No way. I came from a wheelchair. I will make some changes and additions to my wellness plan, but I don't believe I will end up in a wheelchair. This thought is not going to grip me or control me.

I have hope and faith and that is stronger than the push back from the accident.

I trust that all I have been through is meant to keep me moving forward. I am yelling at the accident. You can't have me or hurt me. I am taking my body and moving forward.

One of our volunteers is Asunción. He is the janitor in Wes' office at UCLA. Wes always goes back to work at night and puts in extra hours. We found Asunción reading encyclopaedias on his break. He said that he was going back to American high school and needed to learn English. He had only gone to Grade 3 in Mexico. When he met Haley, he asked if he could help. He became one of our volunteers and Wes became his math tutor.

What a great person. He would get up at seven-thirty in the morning and take his two kids to school, then go to high school himself. Twice a week at eleven-thirty he was at my house volunteering. He would then pick his kids up from school at two-thirty and then work an eight hour evening shift at UCLA. He would go home and check his kids' homework. He told me he wanted to be a good example to his kids. He was a good example to me.

Haley is doing so much better now. Maybe I can start thinking about the future. I know I can't stay locked in the house forever. I have to be well enough to go out and re-join the world. I need to be strong enough to take Haley out into the world too. I am just waiting and listening. I know sometime soon I will know what to do next.

I need shelter from the storm. I believe in the kingdom come and yet I am still running on and I still haven't found what I am looking for. I think that is my theme song, by U2.

"Shadows Are the Illusions of Life" by Fleetwood Mac.

Shadows distort reality. I need to find a reason to come out from the shadows. Please deliver me to my passion. This long and winding road is leading somewhere. I don't know where. I just know that I must stay on the road. Was my road meant to lead me to LA? Now where is it going to lead me? I have learned a lot of life lessons here.

Isn't it weird how everyone is at a different place on the road even when they see and experience the same things? I have bits of clarity to understanding why I have been put on this path. I am trying as hard as I can to piece it all together so that I can see the meaning and purpose behind all of this. I am grateful for the days of understanding. I see the person that I am becoming. I see all the reason for the gifts and talents I knew I had, but didn't understand what their purpose was. I hadn't needed to use them before. I wondered why I was wired the way I was.

I am starting to recapture pieces of who I was before, and who this person that survived all of this was and is. I wish someone else would have been picked. But it didn't go that way. I think there is more for me to learn and more to be revealed in my lifelong journey. I just know that one day I will find my voice and tell my story.

I wish I knew how to kick box. I need to kick box something.

NEW DAY

Each day is another day to move forward and break free from the past. To look forward with anticipation. Never giving up on the future.

The future is ours to see...so hold on. Another lyric from Eddie Money. I am not kidding when I say that these lyrics did not pop into my head before.

Don't stop thinking about tomorrow...yesterday's gone, yesterday's gone. Fleetwood Mac.

I think I picked up a second language. Thinking in the metaphor of songs is so weird. Maybe my head injury turned me into a lyric savant. Is anyone else like this?

I really could have used math skills. I still don't have any of those back at all.

I am thinking about my grandmother all the time. She suffered all the pain of being so crippled with arthritis that she was bedridden during most of her life. She became blind as well. She never complained.

I can't imagine how difficult the conditions of prairie life in a tiny house with little aids, amenities or even a comfortable bed were. She would have had a lot of time to think, pray and meditate on life. I suspect she discovered the meaning of her life and purpose. She is my role model. I gather strength from her every day. Just look how she has affected generations of us. You never know who is looking into the window of your life. We must do our best. We have an effect on others we don't even know. She has guided me to discovering purpose out of all of this.

I think I will smile more. I need to make sure I am looking happy. I keep saying all the positive phrases over and over in my head. The conversations I have with myself are fascinating. I feel like I am reprogramming my brain. I don't put negative thoughts into my head. I need to laugh more.

I keep running every morning and now I can push Haley in a running stroller. What a victory. I am contemplating what all of this journey might mean. Someone complimented me on running up a hill pushing her. Wow, I have come a long way. Today is a good day. I am empowered.

Maybe I can start dreaming about working again. I wonder if that is something I could do. It would be a little tricky with my memory issues but I think I should start thinking about it. Maybe if I pick the right thing, I could do this. I am determined. I wonder who I will meet along the way. I wonder what new experiences I will have in the rest of my life. Can't say that my life has been boring.

Another great day of running. LAPD trains nearby in Westchester. I actually parted their training run during boot camp and ran up the hill faster than them, saying, "Excuse me please!" The training officer yelled at the rookies to try harder. I think they should try harder too. I was pushing Haley in the running stroller and got up the hill faster than those 20-something hard bodies.

Any goal worth achieving is worth working really hard for.

I think my competitive edge is returning. I think this was one of my strengths before. From our yard Haley and I watched the rest of the rookies go up and down that hill, over and over again. I think the training officer figured they needed more opportunity to conquer that hill. I wanted to tell them that it was worth it. How well they run may one day save their life. Running saved mine.

Something is changing inside of me. I can almost taste it. I can sense it. I do not know what it is.

NOVEMBER 1994

Running is becoming effortless. My body feels in harmony with my mind. The anxiety is going away. My intuition has been restored. My instincts have been reborn. I am in the zone. I am beginning to rely on my body. I am having more good days than bad days. This is the first time there has been this switch.

Like a lightning bolt to the heart, I got it. Who knew? Not me, obviously. Now I will have to be guided down this path because I have no idea how to create this. I will start at the bookstore. We three together, begin the journey to adopt more children.

DECEMBER

There is a helicopter right overhead. That means they are looking for someone. I need to get out of here and get home. It is not safe. I could come upon the criminal and LAPD all at the same time. Yikes. Urban running is a tricky sport. I no longer wear nice running clothes when I am out. I wear oversized, very baggy mismatched clothes with dark socks. I put on a baseball cap and very big sunglasses. I want people to avoid me and not be attracted to me. The only time I put on my sleek running gear is when I run at The Strand. You have to have your head up and be watching all that is around you. And I live in a very nice neighborhood.

I can read *Time* magazine now. Victory! This will help me understand my brain injuries more. This has to be at least a middle school reading level.

I am trying to remember to eat. I do not have an appetite. I do not like food much. It seems like such an effort. It is amazing to never be hungry. I think it is a stress thing.

I would really like to ride a bike.

DECEMBER

Order, I need order. Order allows more creativity to flow. Keep it simple. Somehow, all of this is important to how my brain handles all the things that I have to do.

I need to laugh more.

ANOTHER DAY

"All the flowers I planted in the back yard have died and wilted. Nothing compares. Nothing can take away the Blues. It's been many years. If I put my arms around you, nothing compares. I am willing to give it another try, nothing compares to you. Like a flower with

the sun, where did I go wrong? I know that living with you baby was sometimes hard…nothing compares.

Went to the doctor and do you know what he told me. I'd better have fun, no matter what I do, he's a fool. Nothing compares. I am willing to give it another try…nothing compares, nothing compares to you."

Sinead O'Connor's song is haunting me, playing over and over in my head. Does she know me and my life? How can I not remember the names of who I went to school with but I can remember these lyrics? Must be a message! Is this a sign?

I don't think this should be my theme song. It makes me cry every time I hear it.

That's it. When all is lost what do you have?

IT'S ALL I HAD AT DEATH.

It's why I saw and heard everything at death. Our intellect can't make sense of the world and all the things that happen. Our souls help us make sense of our place in the world. When all was gone, the soul was the only thing left. I started life again with just that. That is why everything needs to be programmed back in. I am at the beginning. *"Take me to the river, wash me down, cleanse my soul, put my feet back on the ground. Show me the way."* Now I can hear Al Green in my head. This music thing is very strange. Is this like the new way of giving me signs or what? *"Signs, signs, everywhere signs…."* Five Man Electrical Band.

I hear and see the signs. I truly get it.

I have been swimming again. This helps me work on turning my head and rotating my arms and shoulders. I am so thankful that I am a really good swimmer. This way I can work with the parts that can move and bring along the other muscles that aren't working as well. It feels so good to lie in the sun and let the rays heal my scars. We take Haley in the pool, she loves it. It feels normal. Even our beagle gets in the pool.

The journey is the middle. The beginning was dramatic. It is the middle wherein we find all of the struggles are. This is where we find the greatest challenges. This where we give up or give it our all. To get to the finish line requires stamina and determination.

JANUARY 1995

Busy with all the adoptions details. It is quite a process, but I have complete faith and trust that it will work out the way it is meant to. I just have to make sure that all the people, paperwork and support systems are in place. Stay in the journey and pay attention. I need to be listening so I will know which direction to go in.

Haley's program is going well; she makes progress all the time. We never backslide. She is happy about all that is new.

I am feeling so much better. Heaviness has been lifted from my body and heart.

It was time to turn the page, and I turned the page.

The past is the past. I am building a foundation on happiness. I am changing everything in our four walls. We are not going to be dominated by the past. We have a new beginning. Faith and hope are all around me. Victory is around me. Difficulties are temporary and do not break me down. I have lots of people on my team and we are scoring.

Days where my body hurt are ignored by me. I have more good days. I stay on the journey of doing my best. I am patient, waiting for the children. I know they are somewhere and I can't wait to know who they are. I feel such peace. Wow, what a journey I had to go down to be at this place of expanding my family.

Life really is a miracle. To be treasured always.

Could I have learned all these lessons another way? By reading some books? I like books; I would have listened. Ah, but not my path. I know this now. I have got my helmet strapped on and am waiting to see what happens next. I am swimming with the current this time. What a different feeling this is.

Praying every day for the safe arrival of the souls of the babies.

I am staying in the journey and doing the work. Keeping the faith that the right thing will happen.

My wings are spread. I am in full flight. Running and recovery is effortless. My mind and body are growing stronger every day.

Hey, what happened to all the pain in my neck, arm and back? When did that go away? Grateful. Victory. Points for our team. I just keep on keeping on.

DECEMBER 8, 1995

Today our prayers met. I know where Quinn is, and when she will be born. I am praying for her safe delivery. Stay the course; keep my feet on the ground of the journey.

FEBRUARY 14, 1996

Happy Valentine's Day. We know that Shea has been born and where she is, in China. The time is now. No kidding. The babies are almost home. They are going to be a few months apart in age. Not what I was expecting, but I am not in charge of this journey.

MARCH

Wes has gone to China to bring Shea home. He will be back a week before Quinn is born. Timing is close but we have everything under control. Everyone is ready. We are so excited.

Wes faxed me a picture of Shea. She is beautiful. I can't believe this is happening, such happiness. She is safe and healthy. Praise God.

They will be home as planned. Things are moving along quickly.

APRIL

Quinn is going to be born early. Haley, my adoption attorney Randi and I head off to her birth. I fax a note to Wes' hotel to tell him that Quinn is coming early. I rally friends to be at the airport to meet Wes when he arrives in two days and bring him up to speed. I am off on another airplane to meet Quinn.

The next day we are flying home with Quinn in our arms. She has arrived healthy and safely. Wes is flying into LAX with Shea any minute as well. I have friends waiting to meet me at my gate to help me with my bundle. What logistics. This is just unbelievable. Our army of LA angels are all helping out.

Our planes land at the same time. My friends are talking to each other from their phones at the different gates. They are the only ones that know what is going on. I want to get to the gate to meet Shea. God has a sense of humour because only He could have made this all happen at exactly the same time.

Today the house is full of happiness and two more children.

Cried one last time, uncontrollably, sobbing, heartbreaking cries. We love our babies. We are so lucky. They can already do things that Haley has never been able to do. The life of a baby is so precious; it is not easy to arrive into this world. Life is a miracle.

Over great odds, a long and arduous journey, we were delivered the children meant to be in our family. There always was a plan. I just didn't know it. Haley is so happy today. Wes and I are so happy today. We have a bigger family to love and nurture.

"*I have climbed the highest mountains. I have run through the fields and scaled these four walls to be with you. I have called on an army of angels. I have held the hand of the devil trying to find what I was looking for.*"—U2.

I found what I was looking for. I found joy. Joy removed the fear and sorrow in my heart and in my soul. Joy is beyond happiness. Joy is full of peace, spirit and love. Joy comes from within. Joy developed as I came into harmony and began nurturing my spirit, being in service, sacrificing, loving, rejoicing in austere work, teaching, living in silence and staying committed and determined to the journey I was put on.

I was thrown into darkness to discover the light through the shadows. Joy enlightens the darkness of the soul. I had to learn how to water the seeds of joy so that they would grow. I had to discover all the ingredients in soul food.

It is easy to see joy in Haley. She has had it all along. She has become my earthly guide. All the wisdom I have gained came through my commitment to walking this journey of life, holding her hand.

Haley, my love of you guided me through the darkness to the light. You hold all the answers I had to learn. You are shiny and those that have you in their life are blessed a million blessings. Your gifts are so apparent to all of us who spend time with you. Your gifts have become our gifts. Your sisters are blessed.

Haley 8 years old with her sisters, Shea and Quinn
(Shea is the one on the right)

Emotionally exhausted 2014

BREATHE

...REFLECTIONS

When I read my journal it feels like someone else's life. It seems so unbelievable that all of this could happen. I was having such a great life, then all hell broke loose.

As I started to pull these journal entries out and weave them into this book, I remembered every detail and emotion. I can look at the story and wish I had moved through it quicker. I wish I had taken different forks in the road at different times so that the journey would have moved along faster and I would have gotten to where I am today sooner. But that was not the way it went. It was the prolonged struggle of good days and bad days that led me to the wisdom I have gained and lessons I learned.

The journey was tough. Because it was so tough, I had to discover tools and skills I needed to survive and I learned how to rebuild and restore life. The lessons came from the long recovery, not just the event. It is one thing to survive a life changing event, but it is a different set of skills to stay on the path and not give up as you rebuild life year after year.

I want to say to all the readers of *Breathe*: Let nothing hold you back from rebuilding your dreams. It doesn't matter if there are hurdles or you are not the best at something. If this is your dream, your passion, and it fulfills you, do it anyway. Never give in and never give up. Stay on the journey to renewal and restoration. The lessons and rewards are in the journey. Don't let the circumstances of life write your story, take back your storyline and decide how the plot is going to go. Believe me, if I could do it, you can do it. Look, I wrote a book, how amazing is that?!

BREATHE

...POEMS

I HAD A DREAM

I saw the dream with long flowing hair
Walking up to me as I lay dying

All I had was faith and hope
And the journey of her walking

It had been ten arduous years
I am worn and you are sparkling

In the glory of your Being
My part was always clear

All I had to do was honour you,
And God did all the rest

Colleen Hierath, August 19, 1998

HOLD ON TO YOUR DREAMS

Blessing are small, graces are large
We struggle and bleed for every step
Holding on to the dream year after year
Knowing that fulfillment must be near

When will be our time, dear Lord
We pray and bleed and walk the line
Never to falter and be left behind

How many years 'til we die
Please let time pass us by
And then dear God, you graced us yet
She took her very first step
And then dear God, what we knew all along
This ten year journey was not alone

Colleen Hierath, August 21, 1998

BREATHE

...TO MY READERS

Now that you have read my story, you may at first feel a little drained. Believe me, I get this. Reading my story may have brought up some personal thoughts about your own life. In reflection, I want you to gather strength and motivation to move your life forward in new directions. My story is an example of resiliency of the human spirit. Life is a journey. We can make progress at any point. Our choices may lead us to make left hand or right hand turns. Alternatively, we can completely restart and reinvent the life we want. It does not matter if something has been holding you back for thirty years or three years. It is never too late to be inspired and make new plans.

My life story is about Post Traumatic Progress. Please note that I chose *Progress* over post-traumatic stress. Yes, it was traumatic. But I chose to see each breath as a victory. I made progress right from the start. Before I could even reflect on how traumatic all these events were to me, I was blessed with God's gift of hope. Hope led me to make progress. God was right beside me encouraging me to have hope and faith, and that all things were possible if I decided to come along on this journey with Him. Free will is a tricky thing; I had the right to choose to give up at any time. The decision was ultimately mine. But I continued to ask for help and guidance along my journey.

I know that this is a traumatic story. This experience was bigger than any one human could handle, and I only held on by a wing and a prayer. I knew that God was in charge. It is absolutely unbelievable and I should have died. How does one person survive so many things? And why does one person survive so many things? It is unexplainable unless you realize that I was never in charge. For some reason, all these things had to happen. God really used this experience to make it clear to all who hear my story that we are not in charge. There is no denying it once you have read *Breathe*. It had to be so crystal clear so that no matter what your beliefs, you will see that this was not humanly possible to survive. I was there and know this experience was not humanly possible to survive. Opportunities to grow our faith are presented to us all of the time, but sometimes it takes a great big story to get everyone's attention.

That doesn't mean this was simple for me; after all I was the one in the story. I fought and prayed to understand why and what all of this meant for me. It took this prolonged struggle to recover as well as the harvesting of my faith to find the bounty inside the struggle. It became clear that my life was to mean something more than my survival. I realized my story was a catalyst to understanding that we all have a greater purpose and that all things are possible with God on your side. Don't wait until you hit your big event to find out what your greater purpose is. It would be so much easier to find this out without all the scarring.

I also want to address the issue of addictions. I had plenty of reasons to turn to everything that I could. Never a temptation and never an option! When you have a reason to drink, etc. is when you should stay away from it. No medication could have solved my problems, or changed my reality. It would have simply created another problem to solve. I had enough to solve already.

I also want to address the importance of not being addicted to your problems, situations, stress, pain, helplessness, martyrdom, revenge, blame or circumstances. We are a society addicted to problems. Entire industries have grown over addressing our problems. I refused to be addicted to my problems. If anything, I was addicted to the future, to wellness, to have friends, to have a career, to have a family and most importantly to make progress.

THOUGHTS-ACTIONS AND THE SUBCONSCIOUS/CONSCIOUS MIND

Your thoughts, actions and deeds are crucial to progressing in your life. This is why I chose to look at my journey as progress, not stress. If you go around every day and announce to yourself and the world that you are an addict of your problems, guess what? You will be an addict of your problems. Nothing like reaffirming every day on the stage of life, "Hello world, I am Colleen and I am addicted to my problems." Not going to work. If you go out in the world and think, act and believe that you are progressing, you will attract good things and healthy people. Your possibilities will open up.

To simplify it, just think about the person who complains non-stop about their miserable job. Where are they the next day but at their miserable job? If you think about all the things that you are learning and planning on doing next, then one day you will have a new job. If you think all day about how much your back hurts, then tomorrow your back will still hurt. If you think it is a little better today, that is progress. And then the next day it won't hurt as much. You need to put all good and positive thoughts in your subconscious and conscious mind. See the reality of how you want to be and live. Live in that mindset until it becomes reality. This really does make a difference.

PURPOSE

If you are searching for greater purpose and meaning in life, career, relationships and spirituality, then you need to go deep. We are on this planet to serve others and the greater good in small ways, ways that are not always evident at first glance. Everything makes sense when you do. Your path to your purpose sits in the steps you are taking and the direction you progressing. It is time to make sense of it all, right now. There is no more time to waste wondering what your life is about. It is time to get clarity, to discover your purpose.

Through my experience I discovered my God given talents and gifts. These are the attributes that got me through this life; not my skills and abilities, not my degree, not my work experience. I had to pull these talents and gifts out of the deep and I use them to survive everything and make progress every day. Without them I would have curled up and died years ago. These are the inner strengths and tools to live by. If you want to know how I really participated in surviving, it is these tools. This is why I am here today.

GET SQUARE WITH GOD.

The time is now. I didn't know I was going to die on August 21, 1988. Do you know what day you are going to die? You can't get through life without God and you can't get through death without God. Do not be unprepared; most people don't get a do over.

I did not write this book so that the reader could go "Wow, that was quite a story!" I wrote this to help heal those who need to be healed, to give hope to those who need hope. I wrote this story for the people who are just showing up in life and not being inspiring or inspired. Examine all the abilities, skills, talents and gifts you have and do something really great with them. Get more out of them. What if you lost one of your abilities? I know for a fact it really sucks.

Start inspiring others. Imagine the world if we all lived to the max of our potential. Dig deep and go for more. It does not hurt. Well, it can hurt a little, but you get over it. Affect more people in positive ways in your life. Go after your dreams; your purpose lies in those dreams. Stop being average. Fear has no meaning unless you give it meaning, so use all of your abilities to accomplish great things.

Do you realize what a gift it is to be able to read, understand and remember what you read? You can change the world with these skills.

Find the inspired people to join you along your way so that you can all accomplish great things and affect the lives of others together. You will discover your gifts and talents on this journey and then the journey will move along faster. Be exceptional. Be extraordinary and help others who are moving slower in their progress because they have a few scars. Don't leave the wounded behind.

For the survivors who read my story, know that it will get better. Follow along and gather up all the tools I have used and make progress. Just take it one step and one day at a time. If I can do it, you can too.

PLEASE SHARE MY STORY WITH OTHERS.

Life is a journey and a story that is continually being written. Everyone is at a different place in their story. Please take whatever impact my story has had on you, and keep it for you. Learn the lessons for YOU. Share it with those you think will benefit from it. They will discover in my story what they need for themselves. God will deliver the message they need to hear. Trust God on this. God will do all of the rest.

CONCLUSION

I chose to and worked hard at rebuilding my life. What slowed me down was that I did not have memories of experiences outside of my trauma. I had a lot of emotional experiences in overcoming trauma, pain, and loss. I needed more experience in achieving my dreams and I needed the memories of my previous life. This kept me stuck.

So when opportunity stood in front of me I took it. When a person stood in front of me and offered me a hand up I took it. My emotional experiences of success started to expand.

I wish I did not have to learn all the things that I have the way that I did. But that is my story. One of the important things that I have learned is that there is a very fine line between giving up and moving forward. I have learned that everyone is on their own journey and that sometimes it is through the utter darkness that we see the light of our purpose.

Happiness reclaimed 2015

BREATHE

...ACKNOWLEDGMENTS

Thanks to my children; Shea, Quinn and Haley. You were a part of this journey too.

To my Los Angeles, CA team who came to my home week after week to help Haley survive. The list is endless; you know who you are and how important you are to me. You rallied when I couldn't muster any physical or emotional energy. I could not have survived without you. You changed Haley's life and in turn you changed my life. Tom, Kurt, Bill, Senad, Ascuncion, Tom, Betty, May, Patricia, Margaret, Ellen and Family, Julie and Family, Carolyn, Maria, Natalie, Janie, and the list goes on and on. To all my LA friends who support me to this day...Kara, Vickie, Arnold and Evelyn.

To my doctors and all the medical staff at UCLA; and to my doctors at the Santa Monica Women's Medical Group.

To my attorneys, David Shaby and Steve Cavelli, Randi Barrow, Dale Cockrell, you have protected me at my weakest moments.

To my Whitefish, MT tribe: Linda, Andrea, Andrea F, Sara, Judy, Desiree, Jill, Beth, Stephanie, Cindy, Brenda. Your friendship is immeasurable. You are my sister friends. My feelings for you are deep and everlasting. Your love, support, acceptance and belief in me gave me the courage to reinvent one more time.

To my new Lethbridge, Alberta, Canada friends and Alberta friends, thanks for taking me in when you did not even know that I needed a place to belong. The list is large and endless and you know exactly who you are.

To Margaret, I wouldn't have gotten out of bed without you. Thanks for being there in my darkest days.

To my brothers and sisters and spouses who have been through it all with me in real time. Dennis Hierath and family; Lois Hierath, Chloe and Marv Galts; Ronald and Sharon Hierath; Dawn and Roy Morgan; Margie and Gerard Gravel; Bret and Debbie Hierath; Ramona and Rand Michetti; Thanks to all my many nieces and nephews...thanks all for your love and support. Brenda, Bruce, Jeff, Steve, Andrea, Scott, Teresa, Laurie, Jacqueline, Kristine, Bernie, Remi, Luc, Leslie, Tanya, Brandon, Clark, Adrienne, Patrick, Mike, Nikki and their spouses and children.

To my Mum and Dad who knew how broken I was and how much I needed them. Thanks.

To my Grandmother; who gave me courage to live through the pain and is my guiding light to do good work to this day.

ABOUT THE AUTHOR

Colleen Hierath is a speaker and author. She is the youngest of 8 children, was raised in Alberta, Canada and lived in the United States for 25 years and worked as an executive recruiter. She returned to Alberta in 2010. She has 3 daughters; Haley, Shea and Quinn.

Colleen Hierath Publisher,
Colleen Hierath Consulting
Suite 151 210-12A Street North
Lethbridge, AB
Canada T1H 2J1
colleenhierath@gmail.com